J.2/5

THE TREATMENT OF PHOBIC AND OBSESSIVE COMPULSIVE DISORDERS

THE TREATMENT OF PHOBIC AND OBSESSIVE COMPULSIVE DISORDERS

Selected papers from the Sixth Annual
Meeting of the European Association of
Behaviour Therapy, Spetsae, Greece, September 1976

Edited by
J. C. BOULOUGOURIS, Eginition Hospital, Athens
and
A. D. RABAVILAS, Department of Psychiatry, Athens University

PERGAMON PRESS

OXFORD · NEW YORK · TORONTO · SYDNEY · PARIS · FRANKFURT

U.K.	Pergamon Press Ltd., Headington Hill Hall, Oxford OX3 0BW, England
U.S.A.	Pergamon Press Inc., Maxwell House, Fairview Park, Elmsford, New York 10523, U.S.A.
CANADA	Pergamon of Canada Ltd., 75 The East Mall, Toronto, Ontario, Canada
AUSTRALIA	Pergamon Press (Aust.) Pty. Ltd., 19a Boundary Street, Rushcutters Bay, N.S.W. 2011, Australia
FRANCE	Pergamon Press SARL, 24 Rue des Ecoles, 75240 Paris, Cedex 05, France
WEST GERMANY	Pergamon Press GmbH, 6242 Kronberg-Taunus, Pferdstrasse 1, Frankfurt-am-Main, West Germany

First edition 1977

Library of Congress Cataloging in Publication Data

Main entry under title:

The Treatment of phobic and obsessive compulsive disorders.

Includes indexes.
1. Obsessive-compulsive neurosis--Congresses.
2. Phobias--Congresses. 3. Behavior therapy--Con-
gresses. I. Boulougouris, J. C. II. Rabavilas, A. D.
III. European Association for Behaviour Therapy and
Modification. [DNLM: 1. Behavior therapy--Congresses.
2. Phobias--Therapy--Congresses. 3. Personality dis-
orders--Therapy--Congresses. WM178 E89t]
RC533.T74   616.8'522   77-3384
ISBN 0 08 021472-X

In order to make this volume available as economically and rapidly as possible the authors' typescripts have been reproduced in their original form. This method unfortunately has its typographical limitations but it is hoped that they in no way distract the reader.

Printed in Great Britain by William Clowes & Sons, Limited London, Beccles and Colchester

CONTENTS

LIST OF CONTRIBUTORS

Full names and addresses of contributors. The numbers in parentheses indicate the pages on which the authors' contributions begin.

SIDNEY BENJAMIN (41). Department of Psychiatry, University of Manchester, Swinton Grove, Manchester, M.13 OE4, England.

WILLIAM BUTTOLO (21). Psychologisches Institut der Universitat, Abteilung fur Klinische Psychologie, Kaulbachstrasse 93, 8 Munchen 40, W. Germany.

JOHN C. BOULOUGOURIS (73, 115). Department of Psychiatry, University of Athens, Eginition Hospital, Vassilissis Sophias 74, Athens, Greece.

JOHN COBB (127). Institute of Psychiatry, De Crespigny Park, Denmark Hill, London, SE5 8AF, England.

PAUL M.G. EMMELKAMP (13). Institute for Clinical and Industrial Psychology, Trans 4, Utrecht, The Netherlands.

MICHAEL G. GELDER (7). Department of Psychiatry, University of Oxford, The Warneford Hospital, Oxford OX3 7JX, England.

IVER HAND (105). Verhaltenstherapeutisch Ambulanz d. Psychiat. Univ. Klin., Martinistrasse 52, D 2000 Hamburg 20, W. Germany.

JOHN KINCEY (41). Manchester Royal Infirmary, Manchester, England.

ANDREW MATHEWS (1). Department of Psychiatry, University of Oxford, The Warneford Hospital, Oxford OX3 7JX, England.

LORE MITTELSTAEDT (21). Psychologisches Institut der Universitat, Abteilung fur Klinische Psychologie, Kaulbachstrasse 93, 8 Munchen 40, W. Germany.

ANDREAS D. RABAVILAS (115). Department of Psychiatry, University of Athens, Eginition Hospital, Vassilissis Sophias 74, Athens, Greece.

RON RAMSAY (101). Subfaculteit Psychologie, Universiteit van Amsterdam, Weesperplein 8, The Netherlands.

GISELA ROPER (65). Psychologisches Institut der Universitat Abteilung für Klinische Psychologie, Kaulbachstrasse 93, 8 Munchen 40, W. Germany.

LESLIE SOLYOM (85). Allan Memorial Institute, 1025, Pine Avenue West, Montreal, Quebec, Canada, H3A 1A1.

DEBBIE SOOKMAN (85). Allan Memorial Institute, 1025, Pine Avenue West,
Montreal, Quebec, Canada, H3A 1A1.

BRIGITTE SPOEHRING (105). Verhaltenstherapeutisch Ambulanz d. Psychiat. Univ.
Klin., Martinistrasse 52, D 2000 Hamburg 20, W. Germany.

EDDA STANIK (105). Verhaltenstherapeutisch Ambulanz d. Psychiat. Univ. Klin.,
Martinistrasse 52, D 2000 Hamburg 20, W. Germany.

COSTAS STEFANIS (115). Department of Psychiatry, University of Athens,
Eginition Hospital, Vassilissis Sophias 74, Athens, Greece.

RICHARD STERN (55). Institute of Psychiatry, De Crespigny Park, Denmark
Hill, London, SE5 8AF, England.

WOLFGANG TUNNER (47). Psychologisches Institut der Universitat, Abteilung
fur Klinische Psychologie, Kaulbachstrasse 93, 8 Munchen 40, W. Germany.

FOREWORD

This volume brings together articles which were presented to the sixth
annual meeting of the European Association of Behaviour Therapy in Spetsae,
Greece in September, 1976. All these articles deal with two well-defined
clinical syndromes which have important differences as well as similarities,
but whose treatment has so much in common as to warrant a unified presentation hence this volume. The common aspects of treatment are the employment
of exposure type treatments, though these may require more attention to
cognitive and family complications in obsessive-compulsive than in phobic
disorders, which is well-documented in the contributions by Roper and by
Stern. The syndromes themselves have in common discomfort and avoidance of
defined situations. However, obsessive-compulsives are less bothered by
the situations per se than by the anticipated consequences of being in those
situations, manifest more cognitive elaborations of their problems, and
frequently have repetitive rituals, which are not a feature of phobic disorders.

The papers give an up-to-date account of clinical research in the treatment
of phobic and obsessive-compulsive disorders, and make it clear that clinical
behaviour therapy has moved fast in recent years. Behavioural treatments
are now effective for the relief of distressing disorders which were hither-
to largely untreatable. The treatments can be reasonably brief, and can be
given by a personnel such as nurses without medical or psychology degrees.

Increasingly, emphasis is being laid on patients playing an active role in
their own treatment. This trend is evident in many of the papers, e.g.
those of Emmelkamp, Gelder, Mathews, Roper and Stern. Perhaps many past
treatments, e.g. implosion, desensitisation, shaping and others, all acted
by persuading patients to undertake the key activity of self-directed exposure
to those situations which evoke discomfort so that patients can gradually
learn to tolerate them without their previous avoidance, rituals or excessive
anxiety.

Further research will test the validity of this notion, but the agreement
which is evident among many workers suggests that we are seeing here one
sign of a maturing discipline i.e. the emergence of a consensual paradigm.
Whether this will turn out to be no more than what cynics might call a consensual delusion remains to be seen. However, it is impressive with what
regularity patients are reported to improve by many different workers in
such difficult and formerly intractable syndromes. Moreover, the treatment
procedures which lead to improvement centre round 'exposure' approaches, and
attention is now being paid to the limiting conditions under which these
approaches are helpful for the patient, e.g. the cognitive and social matrix
within which they operate, a point evident in the papers by Buttolo, Gelder,
Roper and Stern. The interaction between interpersonal and phobic-obsessive

disorders is highly complex. This is evident in the paper by Hand, and the danger of drawing premature conclusions in this area is highlighted by Emmelkamp's finding of no correlation between marital dissatisfaction and improvement in agoraphobia after exposure in vivo.

Many issues of current salience are dealt with in various papers. An important one is touched on by Gelder i.e. why for every treated neurotic problem there seem to be many more which clear up without professional help. The answer to this could lead us to more effective prevention. Whether approaches like self-instruction might advance this possibility is not yet known. Research by Butollo and Mittelstaedt examines the role of self-instruction, which can not yet be disentangled from that of exposure. They also find that both group and individual exposure treatment of people with dissimilar phobias can yield significant improvement. A common clinical observation is that patients' satisfaction does not necessarily reflect relief of their problems and this is documented in research by Tunner, whose control phobics who improved least in their phobias were the most satisfied with their 'treatment!

Very useful follow-up information comes from the paper by Boulougouris, that improvement in obsessive-compulsive rituals treated by exposure in vivo actually increases during a mean of 2.8 years of follow-up, confirming similar findings recently reported by Marks, Rachman and Hodgson. Boulougouris also notes that pre-treatment variables which seemed predictive of outcome at the end of treatment did not predict outcome at follow-up. The relationship between changes in subjective and physiological variables in obsessive-compulsives is discussed by Rabavilas. Finally, a negative finding comes from Sookman and Solyom, that aversion relief is not effective in reducing obsessive-compulsive problems.

A mere 10 years ago it was customary for clinicians to draw their main theoretical inspiration from laboratory experiments in animals and human volunteers. Useful as these are, the growing spate of controlled work in patients is rapidly producing a clinical discipline which stands in its own right. This is evolving its own models of more immediate practical relevance to patients. The dialectic will continue between clinical and more basic fields, each cross-fertilising the other, but sophisticated clinicians will need to be increasingly steeped in the literature on clinical experiments which will be the final arbiter of clinical practice. This volume is not intended for undergraduates, but points to current issues for clinical research workers who are interested in present conceptual trends.

Isaac Marks
Institute of Psychiatry, London.

PREFACE

Several interesting topics on Behaviour Therapy were discussed at the Sixth
Annual Conference of the European Association of Behaviour Therapy, held on
the Island of Spetsae in September 5 - 8, 1976. Among them, the Symposia
on Phobic and Obsessive-Compulsive Disorders were of particular interest to
most participants since current clinical research on these topics has been
enormous in Europe over several years. The fruitful outcome of this research
has been most evident from the beneficial effects of the new behavioural
approaches applied to patients suffering from these disorders.

The symposia and the free communications published in these proceedings cover
only the current advances into the treatment of phobias and obsessions. All
contributors, psychiatrists and clinical psychologists are directly associated with the application of behavioural treatment procedures to such clinical
entities. The reader, therefore, should not expect to find analogue studies
or theoretical considerations related to the pathogenesis of the fear avoidance behaviour. The underlying mechanisms of the treatment-procedures presented, which even now are not fully understood, are hypothesized by some
authors.

As a result of the rapid expansion of Behaviour Therapy and the overall increase on many publications in this area, clinicians and research workers
have felt it difficult to keep abreast of the vast literature on their specific topic of interest. It was hoped that the widespread knowledge of the
work on phobias and obsessions presented to this conference would enable therapists to acquire a better understanding of the behavioural methods applied
to such patients and stimulate further research for the development of new
treatment techniques as well as a refinement of the existing ones.

The conference was organised by the Greek Association for Behavioural Modification and Research, under the financial support of the Ministry of Culture
and Sciences. This support is most gratefully acknowledged.

We are deeply grateful to and honoured by Dr. Isaac Marks who has written the
foreword and helped with comments and criticisms on the manuscripts included
in this book. His eminent scientific work is known all over the world. Not
only have a number of colleagues been trained, inspired and encouraged by him
to understand abnormal psychopathology and develop effective behavioural treatment procedures but also a number of them have contributed to this volume.
We would like to thank the eminent contributors to this book who have met our
publication demands without complaint.

The editors wish to acknowledge the co-operation, encouragement and support of Professor Costas Stefanis for helping to apply and develop behavioural treatments in this country.

We thank Mrs. Bessie Livanou for the tedious typing and Dr. Mark French and Mrs. Jennifer Boulougouris for editorial and other assistance.

John C. Boulougouris
Andreas D. Rabavilas
Department of Psychiatry,
Athens Medical School.

1. BEHAVIOURAL TREATMENT OF AGORAPHOBIA: NEW FINDINGS, NEW PROBLEMS

Andrew Mathews

Psychological Treatment Research Unit, The Warneford Hospital, Oxford, England.

In this and the following paper by Professor Gelder, we shall try to give an overview of recent developments in the treatment of clinical phobias, particularly agoraphobia. In this first part I will describe some of the work done in the United Kingdom to indicate the current state of knowledge about effective behavioural techniques for treating agoraphobia, and perhaps provide clues about those variables underlying their effectiveness. In the second part, Professor Gelder will discuss some of the implications of these results and consider that further questions need to be answered before we can gain a more complete understanding of the mechanisms involved.

The studies we shall discuss are concerned with four variables which may influence outcome, non-specific or "placebo" effects, the role of anxiety level and anxiolytic medication, the relation between imaginal rehearsal and real-life exposure in treatment, and finally the role of social factors in maintaining or reducing phobic behaviour.

Our first study as a research team in Oxford (Gelder, Bancroft, Gath, Johnston, Mathews and Shaw 1973) was directed at the role of specific components of treatment, in particular the systematic imagination of phobic situations in either desensitisation or imaginal flooding. On a number of measures, both flooding and desensitisation were found to be more effective than a control treatment designed to appear equally convincing to the patient. No differences were found between the two types of imaginal rehearsal, (flooding and desensitisation) despite the fact that patients felt more anxious during flooding as indicated by higher heart rates. Two tentative conclusions seem to follow from these results. One is that non-specific factors, such as the so-called placebo effect, are unlikely to account for all the changes seen in clinical phobias following behaviour therapy. The other is that short-term differences in anxiety during imaginal treatment do not appear to affect long-term outcome. In both these respects our clinical phobics, particularly agoraphobics, seem to be rather different from analogue populations of volunteers with minor fears. Recent studies with such subjects have produced striking evidence that convincing treatment-like procedures (often called pseudo-treatments) can induce as much behavioural change in the short-term as can desensitisation. Lick (1975) for example, had subjects watch subliminal pictures of phobic stimuli while they were given feedback of progress from impressive physiological equipment. Actually the "subliminal" pictures were non-existent, and the "feedback" faked. Despite this they improved to the same extent as a desensitisation group when given a behavioural test after treatment. Assuming that our non-specific control treatment was equally convincing, it would seem that pseudo-treatments may be more effective with specific fears than they are with agoraphobia. Our failure to find any outcome differences between flooding and desensitisation in agoraphobics also contrasts with analogue studies of common fears, where flooding is generally found to be inferior to desensitisation, at least in the short-term. It may be that these differences in treatment response relate to differences in the nature of the phobias being studied, or they may relate in part to the different time-scales used, as I shall argue later that the short-term effect of flooding in raising anxiety may not be directly relevant to long-term outcome.

To examine this question of anxiety level directly we can look to studies that combine exposure treatment with tranquillising drugs. Dr. Marks and his group (1972) have compared the effects of such combined treatment in patients with isolated fears who were given diazepam or placebo at varying times before exposure to the real phobic situation. They found that real-life exposure had more effect in those patients who had been given the drug some hours before the session, so that the effects were beginning to wear off while exposure continued.

A similar enhancement of treatment effects, this time when agoraphobics were given sessions of imaginal flooding plus real-life exposure, was reported by Johnston and Gath (1973). The design used in this study allowed the separate assessment of drug and placebo effects, and behavioural improvement was greatest when patients had been given diazepam before the treatment session, and were correctly informed of its nature. These two results seem to suggest that tranquillising drugs which reduce anxiety in the real phobic situation can have useful and lasting effects. It remains unclear whether the same amount of exposure has better effects at lower levels of anxiety, or whether a reduced level of anxiety allows the patient to be exposed to more frightening phobic situations, and that this increased exposure is the main therapeutic agent. To determine which of these possibilities is the more likely, we can consider the results of studies in which external limits were set on the amount of exposure that could occur while anxiety was reduced. Hafner and Marks (1976) have reported on results obtained from agoraphobics treated in groups within which some patients had been given diazepam and some placebo, prior to real-life exposure. In this situation it seems that there was no difference in outcome between those patients given drugs and those who only received placebo. One explanation of this, advanced by the authors themselves is that when patients are treated in groups, behavioural limits are set on individual members by the group itself, so that despite differences in anxiety, the amount of exposure was roughly equivalent. In a study of patients with isolated fears being carried out at the moment, we are also finding no differences due to diazepam, when counter-phobic behaviour is constrained. In this design we first find the worst phobic situation that a patient can tolerate, then give either diazepam or placebo, and then continue to expose the patient to the same predetermined situation for a further hour. Under these conditions there is again no superiority for the drug condition, both types of session having a similar effect. The next stage will be to repeat the same experiment, but this time to encourage the patient to do as much as possible in the second part of the session, to test the idea that the drug helps them to face more frightening situations.

To summarise so far, the evidence seems consistent with the idea that subjective anxiety during treatment does not necessarily influence long-term outcome; rather it is dependent on whether or not anxiety reduction leads to different behaviour, in particular to less avoidance. The implications for a therapeutic programme are clear-cut. We should attempt to keep anxiety level reasonably low by, for example, using tranquillising drugs, but use this as a method of encouraging increased exposure to phobic situations. I shall return to these clinical implications later on when considering which components might be part of an effective treatment package for agoraphobia.

So far I have not emphasised the distinction between directed fantasy and real-life exposure. Although it was originally supposed that imaginal changes somehow generalise directly to behaviour, more recently the view has been gaining ground that real-life exposure is the more powerful technique and that fantasy alone has little effect. However most of the studies of clinical phobias which support this idea suffer from one of two defects: either practice was always preceded by fantasy so that the results might reflect delayed carry-over effects, or in studies where order was controlled, only short-term effects were examined. We have recently reported on a longer term study of agoraphobics (Mathews, Johnston, Lancashire, Munby, Shaw and Gelder 1976), in which three treatment conditions were compared; real-life exposure alone, imaginal flooding immediately followed by exposure in each session, or imaginal flooding alone for several sessions followed by exposure alone for several sessions.

The long-term outcome of these treatments was indistinguishable. All patients improved to roughly the same extent. The most direct comparison between imaginal and real-life exposure was provided by the assessment at mid-treatment, when one group had been given exposure, one imaginal flooding, and one a mixture of the two. Even here there were no differences. There were significant differences however between the immediate effects of the two types of session. On semantic differential and subjective anxiety measures patients reported feeling better about phobic situations after being exposed to them in real-life, than they did about the equivalent situations after imaginal flooding. Thus in the very short term our results seem consistent with others, such as those of Emmelkamp and Wessels (1975) showing real-life exposure to be superior, while in the long-term this superiority disappears. Again this result seems to emphasise the lack of direct consequences of reported anxiety for behavioural change, and more importantly, it suggests that some other factor may be responsible for the long-term improvement in the groups receiving flooding in fantasy. One likely possibility to account for the poor immediate effects of flooding is simply that any beneficial effects are masked by a short-lived emotional reaction after flooding. This reaction would presumably not be seen after imaginal desensitisation, and we have evidence from another recent study at Oxford by Dr. Shaw that this is true. A comparison of imaginal desensitisation and flooding in social phobics again showed no immediate benefit after flooding, and a positive change in desensitisation, although once again the long-term effects were identical.

If we conclude that subjective anxiety during imaginal treatment does not directly relate to long-term outcome, then what other factor could be involved? We would like to suggest that imaginal rehearsal, whether at high or low levels of anxiety, has the effect of increasing the probability that an agoraphobic patient will practice entering fearing situations between treatment sessions. Our hypothesis is that there may be very many ways of motivating patients to practice more on their own - rehearsal in imagination is apparently one, exposure during treatment is another, social reinforcement may be yet another - but, however this motivating effect is achieved, long-term outcome depends more on the form and results of this self-directed practice than it does on the original motivating technique. Such a hypothesis while loosely phrased and difficult to test precisely, goes some way towards integrating all the findings so far discussed. From this point of view the

long-term effectiveness of a treatment will depend on it being able to motivate patients to enter phobic situations, ensuring that the opportunity for
such practice exists and that the patient is reinforced for practicing.
Desensitisation or flooding in imagination thus emerges as a surprisingly
successful means of motivating patients to face phobic situations, although
only when that happens in practice are the long-term effects apparent.
Referring to 'motivation' in this way does not of course really explain anything. It is necessary to be much more precise about what we mean before
testable explanations can be formulated, and in the following paper Professor
Gelder will discuss some possible approaches.

To conclude this paper I would like to describe briefly an attempt to combine
the findings I have been discussing into an effective treatment package for
severely agoraphobic patients. Since we feel that the patient's practice in
approaching feared situations between sessions and during follow-up is most
important in determining long-term outcome, it would seem appropriate to
set up a programme which would facilitate this directly. Apart from the
exposure in reality and fantasy during treatment sessions which we think
prompts such practice, there are many other methods which could be considered,
including social reinforcement from the therapist, friends, or the patient's
own family. In the treatment that I will describe, we chose to concentrate
on encouraging the patient's own self-help skills, while at the same time
mobilising support for these from the patient's family, in the case of married
agoraphobic women, from her husband. The reason for this was the belief, on
mainly clinical grounds, that many patients relied on help from the therapist
or clinic, rather than on resources within themselves or their own environment,
with the result that continued progress remained dependent on regular therapist
contact. The home-treatment programme which was developed included several
features designed to facilitate self-management skills, including a detailed
manual of instructions which described the method of facing phobic situations
in graded steps, advice on coping with panic and so on. Guidance was given
on the use of tranquillisers as described earlier, that is as a means of
facilitating further exposure. Since great emphasis was laid on maintaining
motivation for continued practice, husbands were also given instructions on
how to encourage, prompt, and reinforce practice attempts. All therapist
contact was in the patient's own home, and took the form of advice and guidance
rather than active participation in the practice sessions, which were the
responsibility of patient and spouse. Using this format we have found it
possible to limit therapist contact time to about seven hours over four weeks,
with very brief follow-up visits. Further reductions in time may be possible.

Results have been very encouraging. In a series of 12 consecutive referrals
of married women, all couples agreed to take part in the programme, and only
one had to be excluded because of severe marital problems. A comparison of
patients in this programme, and those treated in earlier out-patient trials
showed that the average change by six month follow-up was at least as great
after home-treatment than after treatment by flooding or exposure from the
hospital. Although no claim can be made of statistical significance for this
result, it is of considerable clinical significance since it was achieved with
less than half of the therapist time required in our earlier treatments. In
addition there appeared to be some interesting qualitative differences in
outcome - for example, patients seemed less inclined to look for continued
support from therapists, and gave the impression of increasing reliance on
their own efforts. More evaluative work with the treatment programme is
clearly necessary, but I think we already have enough evidence of its efficacy

to justify some if the ideas which lead up to it. I will leave further consideration of these results and their implications to Professor Gelder in the following paper.

SUMMARY

Recent studies of the treatment of agoraphobia are discussed and some tentative conclusions are drawn concerning effective components. These are that systematic exposure in imagery and/or real-life is a necessary part of treatment, that anxiety level during exposure does not affect outcome per se, although it may do so via its effect on avoidance, and that the short-term effects of imaginal flooding differ from those of desensitisation and real life exposure but that the long-term effects do not. The clinical implications, seem to be that to be effective in the long-term, treatment programmes should motivate patients to enter phobic situations, provide opportunities for this, and arrange that the consequences are reinforcing. A home-treatment programme designed to meet these requirements is described.

REFERENCES:

Emmelkamp, P.M.G., and Wessels, H. (1975). Flooding in imagination versus flooding in vivo: a comparison with agoraphobics. Behaviour Research and Therapy, 13, 7-15.

Gelder, M.G., Bancroft, J.H.J., Gath, D., Johnston, D.W., Mathews, A.,. and Shaw, P. (1973). Specific and Non-specific Factors in Behaviour Therapy. British Journal of Psychiatry, 123: 445-462.

Hafner, J. anf Marks, I.M. (1976). Exposure in vivo of agoraphobics: contributions of diazepan, group exposure, and anxiety evocation. Psychological Medicine, 6: 71-88.

Johnston, D. and Gath D. (1973). Arousal levels and attribution effects in Diazepam assisted flooding. British Journal of Psychiatry, 123: 463-466.

Lick, J. (1975). Expectancy, false GSR feedback and systematic desensitization in the modification of phobic behaviour. Journal of Consulting and Clinical Psychology, 43: 557-567.

Marks, I.M., Viswanathan, R., Lipsedge, M.S. and Gardner, R. (1972). Enhanced relief of phobias by flooding during waning diazepam effect. British Journal of Psychiatry, 121: 493-506.

Mathews, A.M., Johnston, D.W., Lancashire, M. Munby, M., Shaw, P. and Gelder M.G. (1976). Imaginal flooding and exposure to real phobic situations: treatment outcome with agoraphobic patients. British Journal of Psychiatry, 129, 362-371.

2. BEHAVIOURAL TREATMENT OF AGORAPHOBIA: SOME FACTORS WHICH RESTRICT CHANGE AFTER TREATMENT

Michael Gelder

Department of Psychiatry, University of Oxford, The Warneford Hospital, Oxford, England

Although knowledge about behavioural techniques for the treatment of phobic disorders has grown steadily in the last ten years, the response of agoraphobic patients to behaviour therapy is still incomplete. The published reports (Table 2.1) show that the most striking failure is lack of continuing improvement after treatment ends. This is surprising because emphasis is now placed on practice by the patient in meeting feared situations, (see Mathews page 2). It appears reasonable to expect that improvement consequent upon such practice would continue long after the therapist stopped seeing the patient, for the patient should continue to treat himself. Although this is, to some extent, a problem with all phobias (Marks 1971) it is most apparent with agoraphobia. The simplest way to explain this is to suppose that improvement stops after treatment because patients no longer practice meeting phobic situations. Clinical experience suggests that although patients with all kinds of phobia do this, they do not all do it for the same reason. As a rule, patients with simple phobias try hard to continue practice though they may have difficulties in arranging this because suitably graded feared situations are not always easy to find. Agoraphobics do not have this problem; the feared situations are there outside the patient's door, but he does not avail himself of the opportunities for practice. With agoraphobic patients therefore, it might be said that we are dealing with problems of motivation. However the concept of motivation is too broad to guide the investigator and it is better to break the problem down into more specific elements. I shall consider three issues. They are, of course, not the only three, but rather those which we are attempting to investigate at present. They are: the role of cognitive components of anxiety, the part played by self instructions and questions about social reinforcement.

Beck and his co-workers (1974) have drawn attention to the importance of internal language and mental imagery in increasing and perpetuating anxiety. When anxiety leads to rapid heart action it may be followed by thoughts such as "I am about to have a heart attack", which in turn stimulate more anxiety. At other times, the response to physiological symptoms of anxiety may be visual imagery which acts in the same way to evoke further anxiety. Although neither thoughts nor images of this kind are wholly neglected in desensitisation or in flooding, they are not dealt with systematically in either method. It is reasonable to ask, therefore, whether the therapeutic limitations of these techniques are related to failure to deal adequately with these cognitive components of anxiety. It is difficult to answer this question because it is not easy to study cognitions objectively. As a result few clinical investigations have been concerned with these issues. Some work on bronchial asthma comes nearest to the issues, for in this condition, external stimuli for anxiety are infrequent and anxiety is more often provoked by the early symptoms of broncho-constriction. For this reason, the usual desensitisation procedure, which attends mainly to outside cues for anxiety, was modified by Yorkston (1974) who presented instead stimuli related to the symptoms of

Table 2.1   Some results of the treatment of agoraphobia with
desensitisation and flooding.

D = desensitisation   F = flooding

* All results presented as a 1-5 scale: some are from studies
(marked +) which employed a 0-9 scale. For this and other reasons
the results in this column are not all directly comparable.

Authors	Method	Hours	Pre-Post*	Post-FU*
Gelder and Marks (1966)	D	60-70	1.3	-0.4
Gelder et al (1967)	D	30	1.5	0.0
Gelder et al (1973)	D	18	1.6	-0.1
	F	18	1.4	+0.1
Watson et al (1973)	F (group)	9	1.4+	-0.6
Mathews et al (1976)	F	24	1.4	-0.3
Hand et al (1974)	F (group S)	17	1.8+	+0.9
	F (group U)	17	1.8+	+0.1

asthma. Flooding pays more attention to internal stimuli, for some of the
material presented to the patient reflects his own thoughts when anxious.
Watson and Marks (1971) studied agoraphobic patients and compared flooding
using cues relevant to the phobic patients' own fears with flooding using fear
provoking material which had no relevance to the patients' own cognitions.
They found no overall difference. However the material used in 'relevant'
flooding did not concentrate exclusively on the patients' thoughts and images
about symptoms of anxiety. Because the literature has rather little to say
on these questions, we have begun to investigate them; as yet we can report
only the most preliminary conclusions.

In Oxford we are studying patients who present cognitive components of anxiety
as their main complaint. A careful description of these cognitions shows that
it is too simple to think solely of thoughts or images provoked by autonomic
symptoms of anxiety. Identical cognitions can originate spontaneously as
intrusive thoughts. When this happens the thoughts generate anxiety, and they
may also direct attention to sensations from an organ whose activity is not
increased. Thus an intrusive thought about heart disease may turn the patient's
attention to the normal actions of his heart which are experienced as palpita-
tions. Such cognitions may therefore have three effects not one: they "ampli-
fy" physiological symptoms of anxiety, they appear as intrusive thoughts which
initiate anxiety, and they direct attention selectively to specific bodily
sensations. There are also at least three approaches to the control of these
cognitions: distraction including thought stopping, rehearsal of contrary
thoughts, and attempts at extinction either with low anxiety (as in desensitisation) or with high anxiety (as in flooding). We are trying to establish

whether there is any lawful relationship between the form of the cognition and the technique to which it responds. Our work so far suggests that none of these three techniques is sufficient by itself. However, the complexities are such that it will be some time before it can be decided whether they have any specific relationship to the several kinds of cognition. Nevertheless we are encouraged to pursue the work because the self reports of patients with agoraphobia and social phobias confirm that cognitions of this kind are often present. It is important therefore to discover whether the limited progress of agoraphobic patients after behaviour therapy is due, at least in part, to failure to control such cognitions.

Self instructions form the second group of cognitive factors which concern us here. They can be considered either in rather broad terms - e.g. strategies of distraction compared with strategies based on rehearsal of coping behaviour - or in the more detailed terms proposed by Meichenbaum and Cameron (1974) who describe: questions about the nature and demands of the task, answers in the form of cognitive rehearsal, self instruction while performing, coping self statements in the presence of failure, and self reinforcement to maintain performance. Mathews (page 4) has indicated how adaptive self instructions have been introduced as one element in a programme of treatment. When this is done, patients report that these are helpful and that they make frequent use of them, but we do not know whether any other reassuring formula would do as-well. Unfortunately it would be difficult to test the individual components of Meichenbaum's scheme, and we have, therefore, investigated a wider question. This concerns the interaction of coping statements with the effect of exposure to feared situations. Our subjects, all of whom had extreme fears of dental treatment, were allocated randomly to one of four treatment conditions. These were the four possible combinations of: flooding in imagination performed with high anxiety, low anxiety, and the presence or absence of prior rehearsal of coping behaviour. A preliminary analysis of the results indicates that, after four sessions of treatment, patients who heard the less frightening flooding material experienced less anxiety during a standardized visit to the dentist, which was designed as a behavioural test of the effects of treatment. Coping instructions made no difference to the anxiety experienced in this first visit to the dentist after treatment. However when we examined the numbers who had managed to complete the necessary course of dental treatment, there was evidence that coping instructions improved the results of high anxiety flooding, though not the results of exposure at low anxiety. These are preliminary results but they are interesting because they suggest that coping instructions may have their main effect on behaviour after treatment ends - the very point that we are concerned with.

The third issue concerns social reinforcement. Clinicians of many persuasions from family therapists to behaviourists accept the importance of positive and negative social reinforcement within the family. It is, however, important to remember that agoraphobia also leads to diminished social reinforcement outside the family. Thus, friends may be visited no longer and other pleasurable activities are given up. Therefore, one way to attempt to improve the late results of treatment is to strengthen social reinforcement. One approach is to substitute for the positive social reinforcement which is lacking from the patient's family and his life at home, strong social reinforcement from other patients. This is in effect what was done by Hand and his associates (1974) who treated agoraphobic patients in groups in which social cohesion was maximised. The patients in these groups were compared with others who were members of groups in which treatment was the same in every respect except that social cohesion was low. The two groups did equally well during treatment, but only the 'cohesive' groups had improved further at follow up.

These results can be interpreted as supporting the idea that social reinforcement by the group, which continues after treatment, encourages patients to continue meeting phobic situations, and that this is why they continue to improve after treatment ends. Unfortunately, it is difficult to generalise from this important clinical investigation because follow up data were missing from seven patients. It was therefore repeated in Oxford by Teasdale, Walsh, Lancashire and Mathews (1977), who treated 18 patients in 'cohesive' groups and followed everyone for six months. The patients were closely similar to that in Hand et al's study but our patients did not report continued improvement when treatment was over (Fig. 2.1). Ratings by independent assessors confirmed this.

SELF-RATING

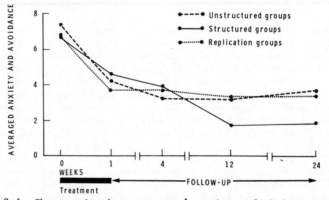

Fig. 2.1   Changes in the assessors' ratings of phobic symptoms during and after treatment of patients in structured groups in the Oxford study, compared with those of patients in structured and unstructured groups reported by Hand et al (1974).

While it is possible that Hand et al's results were an artefact of incomplete follow-up, it must be noted that our patients did not give ratings of social cohesion which were quite as high as those in the structured groups in the other investigation, though they were higher than those in the unstructured groups (Table 2.2). It is possible that there is a critical level of social cohesion which must be achieved before social reinforcement from other group members is strong enough to lead to behaviour changes, and that our groups did not reach this level. It is an interesting point and requires further investigation.

Table 2.2 Mean social cohesion ratings

	Help from whole group	Help from individual patients	Help to individual patients	Perceived liking from other patients	Liking of other patients
Oxford study	5.72	1.28	0.86	2.76	4.58
Hand et al (1974) unstructured	4.0	0.6	0	1.9	3.2
Hand et al (1974) structured	6.2	3.0	1.0	3.4	5.9

An alternative, and more direct, method of overcoming lack of social reinforcement in the family is to attempt to restore it there. This was done in an
investigation in Oxford, which is described by Mathews on page 4. In this,
attempts to teach patients plans for coping with anxiety were combined with
efforts to show the husband how to provide adequate social reinforcement for
his wife's efforts. The therapist visited the home to elaborate on the
procedures which were presented primarily in a written manual. He also reinforced both the efforts of the patient and the spouse, but he did not take
a direct part in the training which was left to the couple. The changes
observed during treatment were rather less than those obtained with the other
methods we have used with similar patients, but the striking finding was the
continuing improvement in the six months after formal treatment ended (Table 2.3).

Table 2.3 Changes in home treatment (H.T.) and Outpatient
treatment (O.T.) compared.

*   difference between groups significant at .05 level
**   at .01 level

Source of rating		Pre	Gain Pre–Post	Gain Post–F.U.	
Patient (1–5)	OP	4.4	1.4	−0.1	
	HT	4.0	1.0	+0.6*	
Assessor (1–5)	OP	3.9	1.1	−0.1	
	HT	3.7	0.9	+0.5*	
Summed Phobic anxiety rating (0–150)	OP	99	34	−4	
	HT	108	33	+21**	

Because the treatment also included instruction in coping strategies, it will be necessary to separate their effects from those of social reinforcement in a further investigation. It is also important to note that, although the total improvement from start of treatment to six months follow up was greater in the home treatment group than with our previous outpatient treatment, this difference was not statistically significant; the significant difference was that more of the change had taken place after treatment ended.

Even this cursory examination of the problem indicates that complicated factors decide whether patients continue to carry out the therapeutic procedures after they have ceased to attend regular treatment sessions. Failure to attend to anxiety elevating cognitions may leave patients after treatment with self perpetuating anxiety symptoms which block further progress. Inappropriate self instructions may also lead to unnecessary persistence of symptoms; and lack of positive social reinforcement may account for some of the patients' failure to carry out the procedures they have learnt. Though they are difficult to investigate, these issues deserve careful study for it is likely that they are of importance in a wide range of neurotic disorders, and not just in agoraphobia. Indeed they may relate to one of the most central questions about neurotic disorder: why it is that for every neurotic reaction that becomes chronic there are many others which clear up quickly and never reach a therapist. It is possible that the factors which explain why patients fail to persevere with treatment also explain why they did not throw off the condition in its early stages. If that is so, our enquiries may be taking us a small step nearer to the most desirable goal of all-prevention.

REFERENCES:

Beck, A.T., Lande, R. and Bohnert M. (1974), Ideational components of anxiety neurosis. Archives of General Psychiatry, 31:319-325.

Hand, I., Lamontagne, Y. and Marks, I.M. (1974), Group exposure (flooding)in-vivo for agoraphobics. British Journal of Psychiatry, 124: 588-602.

Marks, I.M., (1971), Phobic disorders four years after treatment. A prospective follow up. British Journal of Psychiatry, 118:683-686.

Meichenbaum, D. and Cameron, R. (1974), The clinical potential of modifying what clients say to themselves. Psychotherapy: Theory, Research and Practice, 11:103-117.

Teasdale, J.P., Walsh, P.A., Lancashire, M. and Mathews, A.M. (1977), Group exposure for agoraphobia: a replication study. British Journal of Psychiatry: 1977, 130: 186-93.

Watson, J.P. and Marks, I.M. (1971), Relevant and irrelevant fear in flooding a cross-over study of phobic patients. Behavior Therapy, 2: 275-293.

Yorkston, N.J., (1974) Behaviour therapy in the treatment of bronchial asthma. In: Thompson, T. and Dockens, W.S. (Eds.) Applications of Behaviour Therapy Modification, Academic Press New York.

3. PHOBIAS: THEORETICAL AND BEHAVIOURAL TREATMENT CONSIDERATIONS

Paul Emmelkamp

Academic Hospital, Department of Clinical Psychology, Groningen, The Netherlands

Over the last few years, exposure treatments have become increasingly popular in the treatment of clinical phobias. Research, both in analogue studies with volunteer subjects and with clinical patients, seems to point away from such orthodox behavioural treatments as systematic desensitisation, implosion therapy and modeling, towards a basic procedure common to all these treatments: exposure.

However, the way in which exposure is carried out differs. One important distinction is exposure in-vivo versus exposure in imagination. Two recent studies compared the effects of in-vivo exposure and imaginal exposure, both using agoraphobic patients. Emmelkamp and Wessels (1975) compared three treatments in a between group design: (1) prolonged exposure in-vivo, (2) prolonged exposure in imagination and (3) a combination of both procedures: prolonged exposure in-vivo was preceded by imaginal exposure. Results of this study indicated a slight effect after exposure in imagination; exposure in-vivo clearly proved superior to imaginal exposure, whereas the effects after the combined exposure procedure fell in between exposure in-vivo and exposure in imagination. More recently, Mathews, Johnston, Lancashire, Munby, Shaw and Gelder (1976) reported a study in which (1) exposure in vivo, (2) imaginal exposure and (3) a combined procedure were also compared. These investigators however, could not find long-term differences between the effects of treatments involving exposure to either imaginal or real phobic situations, or, to a combination of both. Although the number of sessions and the time interval between sessions were different in these two studies, there may be even more important differences which can explain these conflicting results.

First of all the way in which the exposure procedures were carried out was different. With exposure in imagination, Mathews et al (1976) presented situations from a hierarchy in graded order from the least to the most difficult; with exposure in vivo, items from the hierarchy were also dealt with in ascending order of difficulty. In contrast, Emmelkamp and Wessels (1975) used only those scenes which aroused most anxiety in the imaginal exposure treatment and only the most difficult situations for each client were used during exposure in-vivo. In other words, no ascending order was used. Exposure techniques can be hierarchically ordered along a continuum of approach to fearful situations, ranging from desensitisation to flooding (Marks, 1975). Along this continuum, the exposure procedures of Mathews et al (1976) seem to go in the direction of desensitisation, whereas the term flooding seems to be more appropriate for the exposure procedures of Emmelkamp and Wessels (1975).

Perhaps even more important in accounting for the different effects of imaginal exposure in both studies is practice at home. In the Emmelkamp and Wessels study, no home assignments were given during imaginal exposure, whereas Mathews et al instructed patients to practice at home (that is to say, a

real life exposure) in between the imaginal treatment sessions. Instead of
comparing exposure in vivo with exposure in imagination Mathews et al seem
to have compared exposure in vivo with an interaction of both exposure in
vivo and in imagination. This contaminating role of home assignments should
in further experiments be seriously considered, because of the evidence
from earlier experiments with both volunteers and with patients that real-life
exposure is the most powerful therapeutic factor so far identified.

Therapist controlled exposure or self-controlled exposure.

Emmelkamp and Cohen-Kettenis (1975) found a significant correlation between
external locus of control and phobic anxiety. This suggests that a phobic
patient should not be regarded as someone with an isolated phobia but as
someone who can be characterised by an avoidance of anxiety arousing situations due to a lack of internal control, which in some respects seems to be
the same as learned helplessness. In the light of this consideration acqui-
ring self-control ought to be very important for phobic patients. Therefore,
a shift from therapist controlled procedures to self-directed treatment seems
valuable.

Gradual exposure in vivo with precise performance feedback (self-observation)
seems to be an effective self-directed treatment. This method trains phobics
to reduce their anxiety by remaining in the phobic situation, while they
control their exposure duration to the fearful situations. They may move
out of the fearful situation on experiencing undue anxiety. Recent studies
with clinical patients indicate that social praise from the therapist as in
shaping or successive approximation (Agras, Leitenberg and Barlow, 1968;
Crowe, Marks, Agras and Leitenberg, 1972; Everaerd, Rijken and Emmelkamp,
1973) is not an essential ingredient of this procedure (Emmelkamp and Ultee,
1974; Leitenberg, Agras, Allen, Butz and Edwards, 1975) so that the intervention of the therapist can be reduced. One study (Emmelkamp 1974) with
agoraphobics found no difference between the effects of flooding and self-
observation with minimal therapeutic intervention, whereas self-observation
preceded by a few flooding sessions was more effective than each of the
individual treatments alone. Flooding as carried out in this study, however,
was flooding in vivo preceded by flooding in imagination. Since the amount
of exposure in vivo was not equated across techniques and exposure in vivo
might be more effective than exposure in imagination (Emmelkamp and Wessels,
1975; Marks, 1975) a study which compared graduated exposure in vivo under
client control with prolonged exposure in vivo would be valuable.

Whether self-control adds to the effects of graduated exposure was studied
in an analogue study by Hepner and Cauthen (1975) using snake phobic volunteers
as subjects. Graduated exposure under subject control with feedback was compared to graduated exposure under therapist control with feedback. To ensure
that observed changes in behaviour could be attributed to the self-control
variable, the exposure time of the experimental controlled subjects was yoked
to the self-control subjects. Self-control of exposure time proved superior
to therapist control in reducing avoidance behaviour. One might speculate
why self-control was more effective. One possibility is that a cognitive
process of enhancement of self-attribution of personal competence is associated with graduated exposure under subject control.

Prognostic variables.

While the evidence is growing that exposure in vivo procedures are effective
treatments for clinical phobias, not everyone reacts to these treatments in
the same way. Some patients are symptom-free after only a few sessions of
exposure in vivo, whereas others improve much more slowly, if at all.
Previous attempts in finding prognostic variables for treatment with exposure
in vivo have presented conflicting results and have been generally disappointing.

One variable which might be valuable is expectancy of therapeutic gain. In
several studies (Emmelkamp and Emmelkamp-Benner, 1975; Emmelkamp and Wessels
1975) a positive correlation was found between the patient's expectancy of
therapeutic gain at the start of the treatment and success of exposure
treatment. However, these results are in contradiction with those of Stern
and Marks (1973) who found no significant correlations between expectancy
and improvement.

Another important prognostic variable with agoraphobics might be their interpersonal relations. Several authors (Fry, 1962; Goldstein, 1973) suggest
that agoraphobia is often associated with marital disharmony. However, apart
from anecdotal material there is no evidence to support such claims (Torpy
and Measy, 1974). Another important area in this respect might be assertiveness. The inability to communicate directly and openly with others can be a
serious problem for a number of agoraphobics. It might be important to know
whether agoraphobics with such interpersonal problems improve less than
agoraphobics without such problems with in-vivo exposure procedures.

In a recent study (Emmelkamp, 1976) the effects of gradual exposure in vivo
(that is self-observation), were compared between assertive and unassertive
agoraphobics and between agoraphobics with high marital satisfaction and low
marital satisfaction. Patients were divided in low and high assertiveness,
according to their scores on the Adult Self-Expression Scale (Gay, Hollandworth and Galassi, 1975) and further divided in low and high marital satisfaction, according to their scores on a marital questionnaire (Frenken 1974).
All patients were treated with four sessions of gradual exposure in vivo
with precise performance feedback (self-observation). In between treatment
sessions, patients had to practice on their own. It was hypothesized that
low-assertive patients would improve less than high-assertive patients and
further that patients with low marital satisfaction would improve less than
patients with high marital satisfaction. The results for all subjects are
shown in Fig. 3.1.

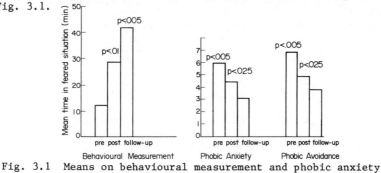

Fig. 3.1   Means on behavioural measurement and phobic anxiety
           and avoidance scales

With the measurement in vivo the client was instructed to go into the street
and to stay outside until he began to feel uncomfortable or tense; then he
had to come back straight away. The duration of time spent outside was
measured by the therapist. At the start of the treatment this period was
12 minutes; after four sessions of self-observation it was 29 minutes and
at one month follow-up, 42 minutes, during which period no further treatment
was given. The significant improvement from post-test to follow-up without
any treatment was remarkable and suggests that during treatment patients
learned a method which they could apply of their own accord. The results
on the phobic anxiety and avoidance scales (Watson and Marks, 1971) also
indicated continuing improvement inbetween post-test and follow-up.

Turning back to the main hypotheses of this study, almost no significant
differences between groups were found. Low assertive patients improved as
much as high assertive patients. Patients with low marital satisfaction
improved as much as patients with high marital satisfaction. Certainly,
this study has to be replicated with other exposure in-vivo procedures before
more definite conclusions can be drawn concerning the role of interpersonal
problems on the effect of exposure in-vivo treatment. Until other studies
are available, however, the evidence so far suggests that interpersonal
problems do not influence the effects of exposure in vivo.

Cognitive restructuring

Cognitive theorists held the view that fear reactions can frequently be
elicited by the individual's label to a given situation. Hence the modification of the label he attaches to the situation can be effective in altering
the emotional reaction of phobic patients. Recently, several cognitive
behaviour modification procedures have been developed. The common approach
in these procedures is that anxious subjects are trained to abandon their
anxiety-inducing reflections and emit more productive self-statements. Cognitive behaviour modification procedures proved to be successful in the treatment of small animal phobias (D'Zurilla, Wilson and Nelson, 1973; Meichenbaum
1972;Wein, Nelson and Odom, 1975), test anxiety (Meichenbaum, 1972) and
public speaking anxiety and under assertiveness (Di Loreto, 1971; Meichenbaum
Gilmore and Fedoravicios, 1971; Thorpe, 1975; Thorpe, Amatu, Blakey and Burns,
1976 and Trexler and Karst, 1972). All these studies however were analogue
studies with students. Unfortunately, controlled clinical trials are missing
at present.

We are now in the process of comparing cognitive restructuring with prolonged
exposure in-vivo with agoraphobic patients. Although until now only half of
the total number of patients in this study have been treated, the preliminary
results may be of some interest. A cross-over design was used Fig. 3.2

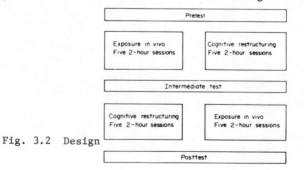

Fig. 3.2 Design

After a pre-test two groups of clients were treated on five successive days
with two hours sessions of prolonged exposure in-vivo and cognitive restructuring, respectively. After an intermediate assessment, there followed a second
period of treatment. Each group was then given the treatment which the other
group had first received. After treatment similar post-test was carried out.
Up to this moment two groups have been treated with a total of nine patients.
With prolonged exposure in vivo patients practised such fearful situations as
streets, shopping centres, buses and restaurants. Cognitive restructuring
was based upon procedures such as relabeling of anxiety producing stimuli
to provide a rational explanation for the development of fear; discussion
of irrational beliefs; and modifying of clients self-statements.

The overall treatment effects for these nine patients on the behavioural
measurement and phobic anxiety and avoidance scales (Watson and Marks, 1971)
were positive. After 10 sessions, prolonged exposure in-vivo combined with
cognitive restructuring led to significant improvements on all these measurements.

For a comparison of the effects of prolonged exposure in vivo with cognitive
restructuring, identical first and second treatment were combined. The mean
pre-post change scores for prolonged exposure in vivo and cognitive restructuring are presented in Fig. 3.3.

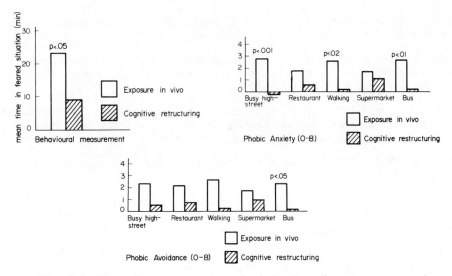

Fig. 3.3   Mean change scores on the behavioural measurement and
           phobic anxiety and avoidance scales.

Both on the behavioural in-vivo measurement, phobic anxiety and avoidance
scales, prolonged exposure in vivo proved to be clearly superior to cognitive
restructuring.

Undoubtedly, definite conclusions concerning the effects of cognitive restructuring with phobic patients can not yet be made. The preliminary results of
this study, however, indicate that clinicians should be careful in choosing
cognitive restructuring as treatment technique for clinical phobias. One

should keep in mind that all evidence in favour of cognitive restructuring is based upon analogue studies with college students; effects of treatments in analogue studies might be influenced to a certain extent by other factors such as demand characteristics (Borkovec, 1973) and expectancy of therapeutic gain (Emmelkamp, 1975).

SUMMARY

Several issues concerning exposure treatments are discussed. Possible explanations are offered to account for conflicting results from studies which compared in vivo exposure and imaginal exposure treatments. Furthermore, research is reviewed which seems to indicate that graduated exposure in vivo under patient control might be a valuable alternative to prolonged exposure. Clinicians argue that agoraphobia is often associated with marital disharmony. A study is reported which suggests that interpersonal problems do not influence the effects of in vivo exposure treatments. Finally, the preliminary results of a study are reported, in which prolonged exposure in_ vivo was compared with cognitive restructuring. Prolonged exposure proved to be superior to cognitive restructuring with agoraphobics.

REFERENCES:

Agras, W.S. Leitenberg, H. and Barlow, D.H. (1968). Social reinforcement in the modification of agoraphobia. Archives of General Psychiatry, 19:423-427.

Borkovec, T.D. (1973). The role of expectancy and physiological feedback in fear research: a review with special reference to subject characteristics. Behavior therapy, 4, 491-505.

Crowe, M. Marks, I.M., Agras, W.S. and Leitenberg H. (1972). Time-limited desensitization, implosion and shaping for phobic patients: A cross-over study. Behaviour Research and Therapy. 10, 319-328.

Di Loreto, A.O. (1971). Comparative psychotherapy: an experimental analysis. Chicago: Aldine.

D'Zurilla, T.J., Wilson, G.T., and Nelson, R. (1973). A preliminary study of the effectiveness of graduate prolonged exposure in the treatment of irrational fear. Behavior therapy, 4, 672-685.

Emmelkamp, P.M.G. (1974). Self-observation versus flooding in the treatment of agoraphobia. Behaviour Research and Therapy, 12, 229-237.

Emmelkamp, P.M.G. (1975). Effect of expectancy on systematic desensitization and flooding. European Journal of Behavioural Analysis and Modification, 1, 1-11.

Emmelkamp, P.M.G. (1976). The role of interpersonal problems of agoraphobics on the effects of exposure in_vivo. (in preparation).

Emmelkamp, P.M.G. and Cohen-Kettenis, P. (1975). Relationship of locus of control to phobic anxiety and depression. Psychological Reports, 36,2, 390.

Emmelkamp, P.M.G. and Emmelkamp-Benner, A. (1975). Effects of historically portrayed modeling and group treatment on self-observation: a comparison with agoraphobics. Behaviour Research and Therapy, 13, 135-139.

Emmelkamp, P.M.G. and Ultee, C.A. (1974). A comparison of 'successive approximation' and 'self-observation' in the treatment of agoraphobia. Behavior Therapy, 5, 605-613.

Emmelkamp, P.M.G. and Wessels, H. (1975). Flooding in imagination versus flooding in vivo: a comparison with agoraphobics. Behaviour Research and Therapy, 13, 7-15.

Everaerd, W.T.A.M., Rijken, H.M. and Emmelkamp, P.M.G. (1973). A comparison of flooding and successive approximation in the treatment of agoraphobia. Behaviour Research and Therapy, 11, 105-117.

Frenken, J. (1974). Huwelijksdeprivatieschaal. NISSO, Zeist.

Fry, W.F. (1962). The marital context of an anxiety syndrome. Family Process 1, 245-252,

Gay, M.L., Hollandworth, J.G. and Galsssi, J.P. (1975). An assertiveness inventory. Journal of Counseling Psychology, 22, 340-344.

Goldstein, A.J. (1973). Learning theory insufficiency in understanding agoraphobia. In: Brengelman and Turner (Eds.) Behaviour Therapy, Urban and Schwarzenberg, Munchen.

Hepner, A. and Cauthen, N,R. (1975). Effect of subject control and graduated exposure on snake phobias. Journal of Consulting and Clinical Psychology, 43, 3, 297-304.

Leitenberg, H., Agras, W.S., Allen, R., Butz, R. and Edwards, J. (1975). Feedback and therapist praise during treatment of phobia. Journal of Consulting and Clinical Psychology, 43, 3, 396-404.

Marks, I. (1975). Behavioral treatments of phobic and obsessive-compulsive disorders: a critical appraisal. In: Hersen, M., Eisler, R.M. and Miller, P.M., (Eds.) Progress in behavior modification. Vol. 1. Academic Press, New York.

Mathews, A.M., Johnston, D.W., Lancashire, M. Munby, M., Shaw, P.M. and Gelder M.G. (1976). Imaginal flooding and exposure to real phobic situation: treatment outcome with agoraphobic patients. British Journal of Psychiatry. 129, 362-371.

Meichenbaum, D.H. (1971). Examination of model characteristics in reducing avoidance behavior. Journal of Personality and Social Psychology, 17, 298-307.

Meichenbaum, D.H. (1972). Cognitive modification of test anxious college students. Journal of Consulting and Clinical Psychology, 39, 370-380.

Meichenbaum, D.H., Gilmore, J.B. and Fedoravicius, A. (1971). Group insight versus group desensitization in treating speech anxiety. Journal of Consulting and Clinical Psychology, 36, 410-421.

Stern, R., and Marks, I. (1973). Brief and prolonged flooding. Archives of General Psychiatry, 28, 270-276.

Thorpe, G.L. (1975). Desensitization, behavior rehearsal, self-instructional training and placebo effects on assertive-refusal behavior. European Journal of Behavioural Analysis and Modification, 1, 30-44.

Thorpe, G.L., Amatu, H.T., Blakey, R.S. and Burns, L.E. (1976). Contributions of overt instructional rehearsal and "specific insight" to the effectiveness of self-instructional training: a preliminary study. Behavior Therapy. 7, 504-511.

Torpy, D.M. and Measy, L.G. (1974). Marital interaction in agoraphobia. Journal of Clinical Psychology, 30, 351-354.

Trexler, L.D. and Karst, T.O. (1972). Rational-emotive therapy, placebo, and no-treatment effects on public-speaking anxiety. Journal of Abnormal Psychology, 79, 60-67.

Watson, J. P. and Marks, I. M. (1971). Irrelevant fear in flooding: a cross-over study of phobic patients. Behaviour Therapy, 2, 275-295

Wein, K.S., Nelson, R.O. and Odom, J.V. (1975). The relative contributions of reattribution and verbal extinction to the effectiveness of cognitive restructuring. Behavior Therapy, 6, 459-474.

4. SYSTEMATIC COMBINATION OF TREATMENT COMPONENTS: SELF-INSTRUCTIONAL TRAINING, MODELLING WITH PARTICIPATION, POST-TREATMENT CARE IN THE BEHAVIOURAL MODIFICATION OF SEVERE PHOBIC DISORDERS

William Butollo and Lore Mittelstaedt

Institute of Psychology, University of Munich, W. Germany.

Within the context of behaviour modification research, the treatment conditions for phobic disorders have been dominated by the so-called two-stage theory of fear and avoidance (Rachman, 1976). Even though this concept has led to new and helpful therapeutic approaches, it may have kept many research workers from looking systematically into other factors that might play a significant role in the behaviour of people with phobic problems. Recently, some of these variables have been investigated in our department (Alt, 1976). One problem was to develop an alternative method of looking at the problems of phobic disorders, how they develop and what factors seem responsible for their persistence. The basic ideas have been formulated within a concept of cognitive rehearsal which assumes that aversive emotional responses are followed by open or silent verbalizations (Butollo, 1976). Briefly, the essentials of this model state that the cognitive (self-instructional) processes, following the perception of aversive emotional responses (e.g. observable as a sudden change of an autonomous activation), are responsible for later behaviour in similar situations. In phobics these self-verbalizations show some characteristics which determine excessive avoidance behaviour and inadequate fear responses. Additionally, it is assumed that these processes are working in both directions i.e. autonomous responses can trigger cognitive rehearsal processes and vice versa, even without any noticeable external stimulus. The reader who is interested in a more detailed presentation of the model is referred to a paper, which also reports some experimental and observational support for this view (Butollo, 1976). This approach has stimulated both laboratory and treatment studies, and two of the latter are reported.

The main questions investigated are:

1. Is it possible to enhance the efficacy of a treatment approach combining in-vivo exposure with gradually increasing item difficulty by including a 'special training to modify what clients say to themselves'- as Meichenbaum would call it - when approaching the feared object?

2. Can this treatment - if provided within a specially arranged form of group therapy - produce the same results as an individual therapy following the same rationale?

3. Does a specially arranged group therapy provide a more effective after-care system?

The first study reported deals with hypotheses concerning question 1, the second study deals with question 2 and certain subjects from both these studies are investigated as regards question 3.

FIRST STUDY: LABORATORY SELF-INSTRUCTIONAL AND GRADUAL CONFRONTATION IN-VIVO

Basic Ideas

Several authors have stressed the importance of in-vivo exposure as an aid in the treatment of severe phobic disorders. Under various titles more or less similar procedures have been used, ranging from reinforced practice (Leitenberg and Callahan, 1973) over flooding, modelling with participation (Rachman, 1969 Roper, Rachman and Marks, 1975), exposure treatment (Marks 1975) and self-control methods in the natural environment (Watson and Tharp, 1975). None of these studies seems to have systematically investigated or modified what clients say to themselves when confronted with their fear situations. In view of other studies, which have systematically investigated self-reports, self-verbalizations and cognitions of phobic patients, this negligence is surprising (Beck and Rush, 1975; Meichenbaum, 1975). The latter authors tried to change attitudes, self-verbalizations and attributions of clients in therapeutic sessions, without including in-vivo training to provide generalization of their treatment effects.

The present study examines the effects of various methods of self-instructional training in combination with a form of active generalization training (modelling with gradual in-vivo confrontation).

Hypotheses

The following hypotheses were studied:

1. Systematic self-instructional training in the laboratory using a slightly stressful but non-phobic situation provides better results than a training for dealing with stress which uses coping skills by self-instructions alone.

2. Stress-training without systematic self-instructional training, shows inferior results than a combination of "coping with stress" training and self-instructional training in the laboratory.

Since subjects in all treatment conditions were given the gradual confrontation procedure, the treatment experiment does not provide an evaluation of the efficacy of self-instructional and stress-inoculation training per se. A part of this procedure, which has been used similarly by Meichenbaum (1975) treating animal phobias, did not prove sufficiently effective in the treatment of severe phobic problems. Evidence for this has been collected in a few single case pilot studies.

Experimental Design (Table 4.1)

a) Factors: In a 2x2 two-way design the following factors, concerning training conditions prior to in-vivo confrontation, have been controlled:

    1. Slight stress, during training in the laboratory, to improve coping skills; two conditions with laboratory stressor present (LS+) and not present (LS-).
    2. Self-instructional training to cope with a stress: two conditions

with self-instructional training provided (SI+) and not provided (SI-).

Table 4.1　　Design and procedure in Study 1.

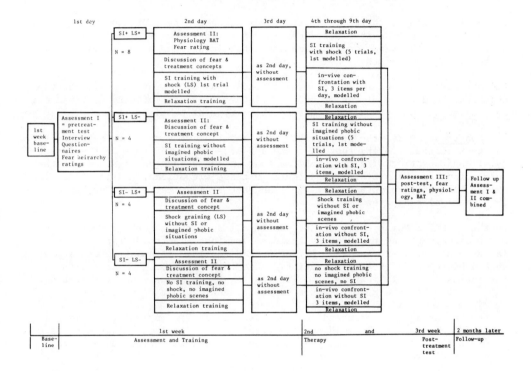

b)　Sample:　The study was carried out in two parts.　The first, which took place during the summer months 1975, included only 8 subjects (because 4 dropped out before the start of treatment), with a second part including 12 subjects.　Total sample size was 20 subjects, all females, with the following distribution on the four experimental groups:

Group (SI+ LS+)　:Eight subjects of mean age 32.8 years.　Six suffered from animal phobias and 2 from situational phobias.　Mean duration of their disorder 15.3 years.

Group (SI+ LS-) :Four subjects of mean age 33.7 years. Two suffered from
                  animal phobias and the other 2 from situational phobias.
                  Mean duration of their disorder 14.7 years.

Group (SI- LS+) : Four subjects of mean age 34.0 years. Two suffered from
                  animal phobias and the other 2 from situational phobias.
                  Mean duration of their disorder 15.0 years.

Group (SI- LS-) : Four subjects of a mean age 35.2 years. Two suffered from
                  animal phobias and 2 from situational phobias. Mean dura-
                  tion of their disorder 13.5 years.

In the first sample therapy, treatment was conducted by four individual therapists, two of them newly trained PhD students. The second sample which
started in March 1976, had six therapists participating, all with experience
as behaviour therapists.

Clients were assigned to the treatment conditions by a staff member, who did
not know the details of the study. He employed several matching criteria e.g.
age, duration and intensity of disorder and type of phobia.

c) Measures: After the intake interview baseline measures were recorded for
one week period. During that time the subjects collected data on the frequency of confrontation with the phobic situation and rated the magnitude of their
fear responses and avoiding behaviours in these situations. Anxiety questionnaires, the FSS (Wolpe and Lang 1964) and the STAI A-trait (Spielberger et al
1969) were also applied.

In the week following the baseline period all subjects met their therapists
for 3 assessment and preparatory training sessions. At the first session
(assessment 1), therapist and patient worked together in constructing a graduated hierarchy of feared situations. The therapist got the patient to rate
the intensity of his fear in the different imagined situations, instructing
him to indicate "how much he would be frightened by that situation".

At the beginning of the second session (assessment 2), physiological measurements and a behavioural avoidance test (BAT) were conducted. A person not
informed about the purpose of the study and the assignment of subjects to
experimental groups took the measures and made the observations. Scoring of
the individually designed BAT followed a simple procedure which counted the
number of subjectively equal steps performed. Additionally, a State Anxiety
Inventory, Form A-STATE, was given to each subject (Spielberger et al 1969).
The assessments were repeated soon after the end of intensive treatment and
again two months later.

The following physiological measures were taken: Heart rate and finger pulse
measures shortly before the BAT. Following a rest period, subjects were
asked to imagine three items out of different sections of their fear hierarchies eliciting low, medium, and high fear, while the physiological measures
were again recorded.

d) Time schedule of treatment: During the first week visits, at regular
intervals, were mainly devoted to assessment procedures and muscular relaxation training which was given to all clients in the same way. Clients in the

groups with laboratory stress (LS+) and self-instructions training (SI+) received their first training during the second and third sessions. All subjects were introduced to the basic rationale underlying the treatment procedure. This introductory process was slightly extended in group LS- and SI- so as to give them equal treatment times. During the second week the clients received treatment of two hours each on five days. They were given another treatment session in the middle of the third week and the post-test (assessment 3) at the end of the week. The first follow-up test was two months later. The second sample was given some special after-care treatment, but this is not finished and will be described elsewhere.

e) Treatment procedures - Selt Instruction (SI): Unlike Meichenbaum's method (Meichenbaum, 1975) the SI was a short text which contained the following four aspects:

1. I feel my fears rising and I accept it as a fact.
2. I compare the momentary threat with a terrible experience in my past which I could cope with (emotional contrast item).
3. I know that I have to learn to deal with this comparatively weak threat/ fear.
4. Therefore, I will actively engage in coping with this situation (e.g. approach feared situation or object).

These four aspects of the self-instructional package can be given, in the client's own phraseology, audibly both during training and confrontation tasks.

The contrast item was included, because of supportive results from a series of laboratory and treatment analogue studies on various aspects of this topic (Butollo, 1971, 1974, 1976; Brand, 1975, Winkler, 1975, Bruer, 1976, Butollo and Werner, 1977 in press).

Laboratory stressor (LS):   The subject was seated in front of an electric shock device. The tasks - the first time modelled by the therapist - was to put the electrodes on one forearm, test the lowest perceptual threshold, increase the shock intensity towards progressively higher levels ("as far as you want to go, but don't forget, it shouldn't be too easy a task"). After a start signal given by the therapist, the client concentrates for about one minute on his "inner feelings" while anticipating the aversive event. Then on a second signal he administers the shock to himself. In the SI+ LS+ condition this self-triggered action, releasing the aversive stimulus is immediately preceded by a rehearsal of the self-instructional thoughts. Verbal reinforcement and encouragement were given by the therapist as well as a short discussion of the client's feelings during the minute while anticipating the shock. This procedure was repeated five times during each session.

Gradual confrontation with phobic item: At the beginning of the first week a time schedule was established for the confrontation tasks during daily treatment sessions. This covered the entire hierarchy of fear situations starting with two or three easy items the first day and gradually moving to more demanding items. The top items were presented during the last days. The therapist had to model each step, encourage the clients to participate, remind them to make use of the self-instructions and, if necessary, encourage them not to hide their fears but to express them and still conquer avoidance tendencies. The therapist tried to create a relaxing atmosphere between trials, mainly by using extensive modelling and a lot of positive reinforcements, aiming at a patient's self-assurance. Confrontation treatment started and ended with a short relaxation period (about 5 minutes each). All subjects received the in-vivo confrontation training.

<u>Procedures in the different treatment conditions</u>.SI+ LS+: Subjects in this group received self-instruction training together with the stressor in such a way that the period of anticipation ended by verbalizing the self-instruction which was, immediately followed by the active release of the stressor. In two sessions during the first week, the SI+ LS+ training was not followed by in-vivo confrontation. During the second week, daily sessions included SI+ and LS+ training followed by in-vivo confrontation with usually three phobic situations per day.

<u>SI+ LS-</u> : Subjects in this treatment lay-out rehearsed the self-instruction package, five times during eash session. Practicing SI with a laboratory stressor (LS) was not provided in this condition.

<u>SI- LS+</u> : This group was confronted with the laboratory stressor without previous training in self-instructions. This condition was included to control for a possible "stress-inoculation effect" by being exposed to slightly aversive experiences - as observed by Meichenbaum and Cameron (1972).

<u>SI- LS-</u> : No training was offered except relaxation and an introduction to the treatment rationale during the first week. Sessions during the second and third week had included relaxation and in-vivo confrontation as described above but no SI and LS was provided. In order to control for a possible effect of "time spent with a therapist" patients discussed recent aversive situations for 5 minutes.

<u>RESULTS</u>

<u>Behavioural Avoidance Test (BAT)</u>

Fig. 4.1 shows the change with regard to the relative percentage of items (steps) successfully performed from pre-test (assessment 2) to post-test (assessment 3) measures.

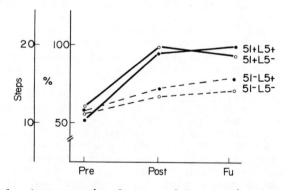

Fig. 4.1.   Average gain of successful steps in the behavior
avoidance test (BAT) from pre-test to post-test
and follow-up (maximum number of steps was 20)

Both SI+ groups show a significantly better improvement than the SI− groups. Furthermore, the SI+ LS+ group shows the steepest improvement gradient. Statistical tests show significant superiority of SI+ over SI− LS+ and SI− LS− conditions (p <.01). The figure also shows that both SI+ groups on the average proceeded to a successful completion of the most difficult items in the hierarchy. This means that almost all subjects of this group performed even the top items in a low demanding test atmosphere! (The main experimental group SI+, LS+ contains subjects with the lowest BAT performance prior to treatment). It is interesting to examine Fig. 4.2 bearing in mind the results in Fig. 4.1.

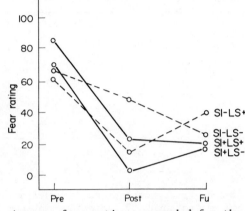

Fig. 4.2. Average fear ratings recorded for the most difficult
item performed successfully in the BAT

This Figure shows the pre-post-change of subjectively rated fear experienced during the exposure to the respectively highest item in the BAT. Even though the two SI+ groups (especially SI+ LS+) showed lower performance scores prior to treatment, their fear ratings for these items averaged higher levels of fear.

Table 4.2   Means (M) and standard deviations (SD) of several
measures; pre-test (PRE) and follow-up (FU); N =20:
(Physiological measures N =12)

Measures		Experimental groups							
		SI+LS+		SI+LS−		SI−LS+		SI−LS−	
		M	SD	M	SD	M	SD	M	
State	PRE	50.8	16.5	44.7	5.69	50.0	5.56	54.3	10.0
	FU	38.8	7.8	34.0	4.24	39.0	2.83	39.7	6.0
BAT 1. successful items	PRE	10.0	7.0	11.8	3.0	11.3	9.6	10.8	8.8
	FU	19.3	1.0	18.8	2.5	16.7	6.7	14.0	8.0
2 fear rating of test item	PRE	85.0	22.0	70.0	20.0	61.3	44.0	66.3	45.0
	FU	19.6	33.5	17.0	17.4	38 3	35.5	25.0	33.2
Heart rate	PRE	75.6	14.9	89 8	21.6	77.2	14.1	84.3	21.0
	FU	63.8	10.0	77.3	6.9	80.8	2.6	72.7	11.2
Finger pulse	PRE	.19	.15	.06	.02	.13	.04	.13	.09
	FU	.11	.07	.06	.01	.23	.06	.14	.05

After treatment, even after performing better than the SI- groups, i.e. successfully completing more difficult items, their fear ratings proved to be significantly lower (p<.01), with no significant difference between SI+ LS+ and SI+ LS-. Average gains in fear ratings of the individually solved top items significantly favor the SI+ conditions over the SI- condition.

Table 4.3 Difference scores pre-test to follow-up averaged for the experimental groups and the main effects SI and LS; S = significance level x p<.05 xx p<.01

Measures	SI+LS+	SI+LS-	SI-LS+	SI-LS-	S	SI+	SI-	S	LS+	LS-	S
State Anxiety	12.0	10.6	11.0	14.6		11.3	12.8		11.5	12.6	
BAT 1.successful items	9.3	7.0	4.4	4.2	**	8.2	4 3	**	6.85	5.6	
2. fear rating of test item	65.4	53.0	22.9	41.3	**	59.2	32.1	**	44.2	47.2	
Heart rate	11.8	12.5	-3.6	11.6	**	12.2	7.6	**	4.1	12.0	**
Finger pulse	0.08	0.00	-0.10	-0.01	*	.04	-.06	*	-.01	-.01	

Hierarchy ratings

Fifteen items of the fear hierarchy were rated on a scale ranging from 0 to 100, with 0 representing no fear and 100 indicating maximum fear. In Fig.4.3 the individual scores are averaged in two ways, (a) items within individual hierarchies and (b) across subjects within groups.

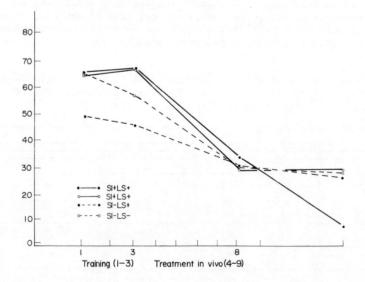

Fig. 4.3 Average hierarchy ratings recorded during assessment, training and treatment sessions as well as during the post-test

The absolute pre-treatment scores were similar for three groups (SI+ LS+ SI+ LS-, and SI- LS-), but were significantly lower for the other group (SI- LS+). The main experimental group (SI+ LS+) showed statistically highly significant improvement between pre- and post-test measures. The other three groups showed significant improvement but less than that of group IS+ LS+. Statistical tests using absolute scores show the significant superiority of the SI+ LS+ group at the post test. Significance tests for differences show the same result.

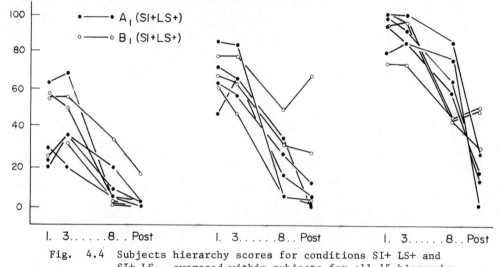

Fig. 4.4   Subjects hierarchy scores for conditions SI+ LS+ and
            SI+ LS-, averaged within subjects for all 15 hierarchy
            items

Figs. 4.4 and 4.5 show average scores for the three different sub-sections of hierarchy, i.e. a grouping of the easy, medium and difficult items. Averages have been calculated within subjects (second sample only).

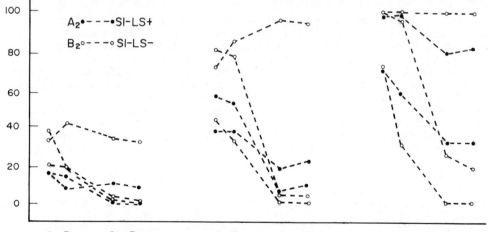

Fig. 4.5   Subjects hierarchy scores for conditions SI- LS+ and SI-
            LS-, averaged within subjects for all 15 hierarchy items

Fig. 4.4 shows individual curves for subjects in groups SI+ LS+ and SI+ LS-,
and Fig. 4.5 for SI- LS+ and SI- LS-. These figures nicely demonstrate that
subjects in the SI+ LS+ condition show the highest improvement rates, especially in the sub-section with the most difficult items. Fig. 4.6 shows
averages over subjects within treatment groups but separated for the three
hierarchy sections. Again, superiority of SI+ LS+ is shown more clearly for
the most difficult sub-section of the hierarchy.

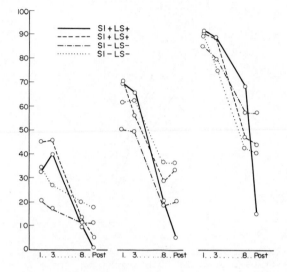

Fig. 4.6   Average hierarchy ratings (0-100) drawn separately
           for the lower, medium and upper section of the
           hierarchy.

Conclusions

The results are not due to the experimental variations only. The highly
significant improvement in all four groups is also due to relaxation training
and especially to the modelling and the in-vivo confrontation treatment.
However, the differential effectiveness of the four treatments is most probably due to the experimentally controlled variables of specific self-instructions and the laboratory stress training. Maybe there is also a statistical
interaction between the treatments which were the same for all subjects and
the treatments which were specific for the experimental groups. However, it
was not a purpose of this study to disentangle such treatment factors. The
study was aimed at an improvement of treatments which consisted of single
components like self-instructions or stress inoculation only. They seemed
somewhat incomplete, even though their relative efficacy has been suggested
by some analogue studies.

This study was designed to isolate and systematically to investigate certain
important variables, of a total "treatment package", consisting of relaxation
training, modelling, in-vivo confrontation with graduated approximation as
well as self-instruction training. It can be concluded from the results
that this package treatment appears very successful procedure in the treatment

of phobic disorders. It is also concluded that a special form of systematic
self-instruction training including a modest non-phobic laboratory stressor,
impressively improves the efficacy of the treatment program. However, it
must be remembered that the SI+ LS- group also had some exposure in imagination during the training procedures. Consequently, superior results could
be expected. This is not so for SI+ LS+ because, in this condition, the
exposure in imagination was not given and therefore this group should resemble
the SI- groups in this aspect.

The procedure seems to provide a useful tool for clients to learn how to
perceive their fears not in an all-or-none fashion - as they usually do -
but in a gradually varying set of responses which they can control within
certain limits. It should help them effectively to identify and change their
avoidance strategies, especially in the critical periods of increasing aversive emotions.

Further research must investigate the question of differential efficacy of
the treatment depending on the type of fear problems to be cured, e.g. animal
phobias versus agoraphobias, versus various anxiety neurosis or so-called
free-floating anxieties. Other problems to be investigated are concerned
with after-treatment care. The subjects of the second sample are in a special
therapeutic arrangement for post-treatment care, where the therapist is gradually withdrawing his interventions but leaving the patients with certain
tools to help themselves in an organized way. A pilot study, which the
authors performed together with two students, should provide information about
the possibility of using behaviourally oriented group techniques for the
treatment of phobic patients. A special combination of self-instruction, in-
vivo confrontation and structure group activities has been employed. However,
experimental control was attempted for self-instructional variables and structured group avtivities. The latter also included activities outside of
treatment sessions. A short report of this study is given below.

SECOND STUDY: GROUP TREATMENT WITH PHOBIC PATIENTS INCLUDING SELF-INSTRUCTIO-
               NAL TRAINING AND MUTUAL ASSISTANCE BY PATIENTS AS FELLOW-
               THERAPISTS

Previous studies, using behaviourally oriented group therapy for phobic patients, have either applied systematic desensitization in groups - which is
not a group therapy in the usual sense - or have used homogenous groups with
regard to the emotional problem (Hand et al, 1974). There were three main
aspects in the rationale for this study:

1. If phobic subjects within a therapeutic group have, respectively different
    sources of fears and different feared objects, a better modelling situa-
    tion can be expected. If, for example, a person with excessive fear of
    snakes can observe the irrational fears of an agoraphobic person, he will
    have a better chance to understand the mechanisms of such responses (in-
    cluding his own) than if he were watching another snake phobic, because
    the agoraphobic situation is not an aversive situation for this person.

2. In-vivo confrontation training could be supervised, after the therapist's
    introductory modelling, by another patient from the same group. Pairs
    of patients could practice treatment steps by supervising each other's
    in-vivo confrontations. This could allow a reduction in the number of

expert-controlled therapeutic sessions, without loss of efficacy.

3. Some aspects of group therapy can be effective in addition to the specific
    treatment components. Among others are, talking about phobic as well as
    non-phobic problems with "yoke-fellows", having more social contact, more
    realistic modelling conditions and the successful change in another pa-
    tient is more convincing than the therapist's persuasion.

Again, as in the study already reported, a "treatment package" has been used
and a few variables have been controlled experimentally. Therefore, overall
success cannot be ascribed to experimental variations alone. In future treatment packages, group treatment is expected to take its place within a sequence
of treatments, which could begin with intensive individual training, as described in the first study, followed by group treatments and patients self-organi-
sed help at the end. However, for this pilot study it was designed to study
the effect of group treatment on its own. This could allow us the relative
efficacy of individual and group methods to be estimated before using them
together in one treatment package.

Hypotheses:

1. Is there a facilitative effect, if pairs of patients from a therapeutic
    group work together on the solution of their problems? They could, for
    instance, talk about various topics of the treatment between sessions
    and participate, as each other's supervisors, in some form of "home treat-
    ment", especially with regard to in-vivo confrontation exercises.

2. Can the use of specific self-instructions, in combination with in-vivo
    confrontation exercises, increase therapeutic efficacy?

3. Does behavioural group therapy, which includes highly structured as well
    as less structured sessions, show the same effects as individual treatment
    which applies the same behavioural techniques but does not provide the
    group effects?

Experimental Design

a) Factors: A 2x2 design was used with four experimental cells all having
group treatment. Additionally, a control group was included as a fifth cell,
in which the subjects received individual treatment. For the group treatment
two factors were controlled:

1. Systematic self-instructional training, using the same elements as in the
    first study, but with the non-phobic laboratory stress omitted. This ex-
    perimental condition was similar to the training procedure SI+ LS- of
    the earlier study. The two levels of the experimental factor were self-
    instructional training offered (SI+) and not offered (SI-).

2. Group members "pair off" to meet between sessions ("treatment partner")
    supervise each other's in-vivo confrontation exercises, arrange to go to
    social events together and provide help in various ways for each other.
    The two levels of the factor were group with "treatment partners" (TP+)
    versus group without "treatment partners"(TP-).

Several aspects of the treatment were the same for all five treatment conditions:

1. Relaxation training together with the assessment sessions prior to treatment and at the beginning and end of each treatment.

2. Introductory discussion about treatment rationale and some topics from the psychology of learning, e.g. avoidance learning, negative reinforcement effects and extinction by response prevention.

3. In-vivo confrontation training as an important part of all therapeutic sessions.

The following aspects were the same for the four group therapy conditions but not for the control subjects receiving individual treatment:

1. All group members had discussions about their social behaviour, especially verbal behaviour about their fears.

2. Possible rewarding effects of their fear with regard to social consequences were discussed at some length (social reinforcement of their fears by family members). The possibility was pointed out that their phobic behaviour might be rewarded by other family members for altruistic reasons or a desire to control the patient. Patient's reports about family members' responses to their home exercises were used for this purpose.

3. Causes for relapses were discussed, e.g. fatalistic causal attributions after a "bad day", the most likely course of a fluctuating type of improvement etc.

b) Sample: Twenty seven carefully selected clients with severe chronic fears of various objects and situations, participated, including some with multiple phobic problems. Patients with free floating anxiety or dominating non-phobic symptoms were not included. Clients were recruited from a group, who answered to an advertisement in a local paper.

Matching of subjects to groups was based on several criteria such as; type of dominating fears, duration of problem, age and sex.

Distribution in the groups was the following:

1. Group treatment

Group SK+ TP+: Six subjects mean age 37.2 years. Two suffered from animal phobias and 4 from situational phobias. Mean duration of the disorder was 20.5 years. Four were females and 2 males.

Group SK+ TP-: Five subjects of mean age 35.6 years. Two suffered from animal phobias and another three from situational phobias. Mean duration of the disorder was 23.8 years. Four were females and one male.

Group SK- TP+: Six subjects of mean age 35 years. Two suffered from animal phobias and 4 from situational phobias. Mean duration of the disorder was 12.7 years. Five were females and 1 male.

Group SK- TP- : Four subjects of mean age 33.8 years. One suffered from animal phobias and 3 from situational phobias. Mean duration
of the disorder was 12.5 years. All were females.

2.   Individual treatment

Group SK- TP- : Four subjects of mean age 37.3 years. Two suffered from animal phobias and 2 from situational phobias. Mean duration
of disorder was 27.5 years. All were females.

Assignment to the cells was done by a staff member who did not know the details of the treatment conditions. Each of the five groups was planned to
consist of six patients in order to keep the group size during sessions mana-
geable. Two clients dropped out during treatment; one a severe agoraphobic
woman with marked marital problems and the other a claustrophobic woman, in
whom other severe problems arose during the course of treatment and she felt
she had to deal with them first.

c)   Measures: For the various steps of the assessment the same measures were
used as in the first study, i.e. behavioural avoidance test (BAT), hierarchy
ratings, FSS (Wolpe and Lang 1964), self-observation of phobic responses in-
vivo (baseline) and checklist for a subjective evaluation of anxiety levels
for imagined phobic situations. These measures were applied both during pre-
and post-tests. Furthermore, fear hierarchy ratings were recorded at the
beginning of each treatment session.

d)   Time schedule of treatment: After the assessment phase, group sessions
were offered twice a week for a period of two weeks, followed by one session
per week for a period of four weeks. After a break of one month (Christmas
holidays) therapy sessions were then gradually faded out. During that period
meetings were arranged first with a two weeks' interval, then with a three
weeks' interval and the last one after an interval of four weeks. The number
of group therapy sessions totaled eleven. After the post-tests, monthly
meetings were arranged but with no therapists participating as group leaders.
Individually treated clients were given the same time schedule for the first
two months but the fading out of the therapists occurred faster and no meetings were arranged for clients only.

e)   Treatment procedures - Group treatment: Self-instructional training
followed closely the procedure used in the SI+ LS- condition of the earlier
study, except that it was performed in groups of six clients. The different
steps of a group session were always in the same time schedule. A typical
session was as follows:

1.   Muscle relaxation (approximately 10 minutes).
2.   Hierarchy ratings (5 minutes).
3.   Discussion of experiences since the last meeting, especially home-work
      exercises. This included the work of the "treatment partner" and the use
      of self-instructions in critical situations. Social rewards for progress
      were provided extensively by therapists and fellow-clients.
4.   Discussions followed on one of the topics mentioned above. These included

the role of verbal behaviour in the stabilization of phobic behaviour, the role of family members or other significant persons in the patients' social environments or socially tolerable ways of expressing negative feelings (30 minutes).
5. Setting up in-vivo confrontation for each patient for the session, discussion of the home-work assignment of each patient for the days between sessions and rating the subjective difficulty or anticipated level of anxiety assigned to that exercise (fear thermometer).
6. Muscle relaxation and practice in imagination.
7. Actual performance of the in-vivo confrontation with the help of a therapist, a co-therapist or a "treatment partner".

In each group session, one therapist and one or two co-therapists were present. At the end of the program presence of the therapist gradually faded out.

Individual treatment

Relaxation, treatment rationale, in-vivo confrontation and home exercises were similar to the group therapy methodology except that there was more time for in-vivo confrontations per client and session. Discussions, similar to step (4) of the group therapy treatment were shorter. No systematic self-instructional training and no "therapy partner" were provided.

RESULTS

Behavioural Avoidance Tests

Table 4.4 shows the average difference between the pre- and post-tests, i.e. the average gain in avoidance steps performed successfully out of a range of fifteen steps.

			Self-instruction (SI)		Control (individual tr, 1T)
			SI+	SI-	
	TP+	I	5.0	-4.0	2.5
		II	36	18	42
		III	40	16	16
Treatment		IV	37	26	55
Partner		V	30	11	55
(TP)	TP-	I	-4.0	2.3	
		II	26.6	28	
		III	30	31	
		IV	27	26	
		V	21	24	

Significance tests: IT < SI - TPt, SI - TP-, SI + TP- (p< .01) but not in SI + TP + for measures I, II, IV, V.

SI + TP + < other group therapy conditions in I (< .01), II (< .05), IV (< .05),

Table 4.4 shows the average difference between the pre- and post-tests, i.e. the average gain in avoidance steps performed successfully out of a range of fifteen steps. The main experimental group (SI+ TP+) shows the best improvement, but only the difference in the three other group treatments appears statistically significant. This significance cannot be found between (SI+TP+) and the control group with individual treatment.

Hierarchy ratings

The change in average hierarchy ratings is shown in Fig. 4.7.

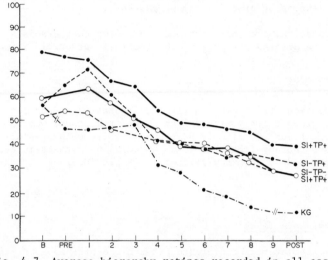

Fig. 4.7 Average hierarchy ratings recorded in all assessment and treatment sessions; B = baseline, PRE = pretest, and POST =Post test

All groups show considerable improvement and it can be seen that at the start of the program, the main experimental group has the highest average scores. This makes the interpretation of absolute ratings difficult.

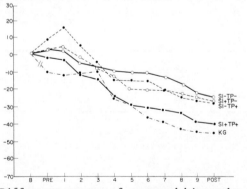

Fig. 4.8 Difference scores of averaged hierarchy ratings:Xo- XI; Xo=baselinescore;XI =scores from assessment or treatment sessions

Fig. 4.8 shows difference scores, i.e. the average group ratings are seen relatively to their mutual scores: XI - XO. This gives a better view of the changes that occurred during the course of the treatment program. Table 4.4 shows overall pre- and post-test changes for the five groups as well as after separation into easy, medium and difficult sections of the hierarchy. It can be seen that the main experimental group (SI+ TP+) in all measures exceeds other groups, except the group with individual training. The latter is superior for the medium and difficult items but not for the easier ones.

CONCLUSIONS

The results show appreciable improvements for the group therapies and the individual therapy. The specially arranged group therapy, with self-instructional training and a "treatment partner" concept, can produce similar effects as individual therapy. If the results are compared with those of the fairly massed individual training, used in the previous study, they do not appear so convincing. In particular, the differential effect of the treatments, for easy and difficult items i.e. low and high fear arousing situations suggest that a start is made with individual therapy, as described in the first study. After some success has been achieved, preparations should be made for a group therapy similar to the one used. This should help clients to improve further and especially to gain more self-control and social skills. The latter aspects should provide a better generalization of the successes gained during individual treatment. It should prepare the client with skills to help them deal with temporary relapses. Such incidents might occur even in certain very successful cases. If clients can overcome such usually short critical periods, this should protect them from disastrous experiences. A "treatment partner" with a similar background of experiences, well learned positive self-instructions in view of a stressful event and the knowledge of his ability to cope with the problem should be able to assist the client, even in very distressing periods. The two treatment approaches are now employed in a new study which combines the individual and group treatments. Special attention is given to the fade out of the therapist and the organization of a self-control system that enables patients to keep in contact later and provides them with some therapeutic skills. Hopefully, forthcoming results will teach more about such problems. Future research should also concentrate on differential applicability and effectiveness of the treatment package for different types of anxiety patients, a question which has been neglected in the studies reported here, in so far as systematic experimental control is concerned.

ACKNOWLEDGEMENTS

We are grateful to Elisabeth Hoffner and Ursula Munch, who worked as therapists with the first sample together with the authors. We also express our thanks to Hanne Dirlich-Wilhelm, Gisela Roper and Andrea Werner, Angelika Bastin and Ulrike Schluter for participating as therapists.

REFERENCES

Alt, B. (1976). Kognitive Variablen der Angstkontrolle - Eine experimentelle Untersuchung. Diplomarbeit, Universitat Munchen.

Beck, A.T., and Rush, A.J. (1975). A cognitive model of anxiety formation and anxiety resolution. In SARASON, I.G. and SPIELBERGER, C.D. (Eds.) Stress and Anxiety, Vol. 2, 69-80.

Brand, J. (1975). Kontexteffekte bei Emotionen. Diplomarbeit, Universitat, Munchen.

Bruer, J. (1976). Anwendung der Adaptationstheorie auf die Therapie von Phobien. Diplomarbeit, Universitat Munchen.

Butollo, W.H. (1971). Stimulus relations in classical GSR conditioning. Psychonomic Science, 23, 401-403.

Butollo, W.H. (1974). Experimente zur Modifikation aversiver Emotionen. Verband wissenschaftlicher Gesellschaften Osterreichs, Wien.

Butollo, W.H. (1976). Psychologische Therapien extremer chronischer Angstreaktionen. Paper read at the German Psychology Conference, Regensburg.

Butollo, W.H. and Werner, A. (1977). A forced extinction of GSR responses using response prevention and contrast stimulation in human subjects. Behaviour Research and Therapy, (in press).

Hand, I., Lamontagne, Y., and Marks I.M. (1975). Group exposure (flooding) in-vivo for agoraphobics. British Journal of Psychiatry, 124, 588-602.

Leitenberg, H. and Callahan, E.J. (1973). Reinforced practice and reduction of different kinds of fears in adults and children. Behaviour Research and Therapy, 11, 19-30.

Marks, I. (1975). Modern trends in the management of morbid anxiety: Coping stress immunization and extinction. In: SPIELBERGER, C.D. and SARASON, I.G. (Eds.) Stress and Anxiety, Vol. 1, 213-235.

Meichenbaum, D., (1975). A self-instructional approach to stress management: A proposal for stress inoculation training. In: SPIELBERGER, C.D. and SARASON I.G. (Eds.) Stress and Anxiety, Vol. 1, 237-263.

Meichenbaum, D. and Cameron, R., (1972). Stress inoculation: A skills training approach to anxiety management. Unpublished manuscript. University of Waterloo, Ontario.

Rachman, S., (1969). Treatment by prolonged exposure to high intense stimulation. Behaviour Research and Therapy, 7, 295-302.

Rachman, S. (1976). The passing of the two-stage theory of fear and avoidance: fresh possibilities. Behaviour Research and Therapy, 14, 125-131.

Roper, G., Rachman, S., and Marks I., (1975). Passive and participant model-ling in exposure treatment of obsessive-compulsive neurotics. Behaviour Research and Therapy, 13, 271-279.

Spielberger, C.D., Gorsuch, R.N. and Lushene, R.E. (1969). Test Manual for form X, Cons. Psychologists Press, Palo Alto.

Watson, D. and Tharp, R., (1975). Self-directed behaviour: Self-modification for personal adjustment. Brooks/Cole Publishing Co., Belmont, (German edition Pfeifferm Munchen).

Winkler, B. (1975). Experimentelle Untersuchung zur Frage von Kontexteffekten auf die Beurteilung aversiver Selbstverbalisationen. Diplomarbeit, Universi-tat Munchen.

Wolpe, M. and Lang, P.J., (1964). A fear survey schedule for use in behaviour therapy. Behaviour Research and Therapy, 2, 27-30.

5. THE TREATMENT OF AGORAPHOBIA: SKILL OR TECHNIQUE?

Sidney Benjamin and John Kincey

Department of Psychiatry, Manchester University, England

INTRODUCTION

The development of behavioural treatments for the phobic neuroses was initiated by psychologists and their approach has gained widespread acceptance by psychiatrists. More recently the need for behaviour therapists has resulted in the training of nurses who can assess and treat a range of disorders using behavioural treatments (Marks et al in press). Training of staff, whether they be psychologists, psychiatrists or nurses in the use of behavioural methods is becoming a highly complex, prolonged and expensive matter, and post-graduate training commonly lasts between one and two years. Whilst the training of highly skilled therapists in increasing numbers may be desirable, it seems unlikely that it will be possible to train sufficient people to meet the clinical demands within the foreseeable future.

It is difficult to make an accurate assessment of the numbers of disabled phobic subjects. Most surveys of psychiatric patients show between 2% and 4% to be phobic and a community survey suggests that only about one quarter of phobics may be treated (Agras, Sylvester and Oliveau, 1969). Amongst those who are treated it is apparent that for many the treatment is unsuccessful. For example, the majority of the 1200 agoraphobic responders in the 'Open Door' survey had received treatment but continued to be disabled (Marks and Herst, 1970). It is apparent that there is a need for more effective treatment to be available for these disabled people. There is ample evidence that various forms of behaviour therapy are highly effective in the management of phobias when applied by skilled workers but available treatment is insufficient to meet the needs of the community.

It is against this background that we have been considering the possibility of providing effective treatment for the many patients to whom skilled behaviour therapy is not yet available. One possibility appears to be the use of larger numbers of therapists who have only the briefest of training. In this case it seems unlikely that they would be able to acquire a detailed grasp of the underlying concepts, to carry out an analysis of the disability to be treated, nor to plan the exact requirements of individual treatments. Such therapists might be trained to simply carry out a predetermined technique for patients previously selected as suitable for such treatment. The questions we are asking are:

1.　What form should such treatment take?
2.　How much training is essential for the therapist?
3.　For which patients is it suitable?
4.　Can it be as effective as the best treatments currently available?

It is to try and answer some of these questions that we have started a clinical study of such treatment which might be expected to be effective in the light of recent research.

METHOD

Subjects are patients who have been initially referred by general practitio-
ners or other doctors. At out patient assessment they have been found to
have agoraphobia sufficiently severe to seriously impair their social and
occupational function, and there has been no evidence of a primary mood
disorder.

Treatment. If the patient has been on psychotropic medication this has been
stopped in the course of the first week after admission to the unit.

The behavioural treatment programme forms the central aspect of their management. This is divided into three 'modules', each of which deals with one
aspect of the situations commonly feared by agoraphobics. These are:

1.   Walking outside the unit, which is located in an inner suburb
     of the city.
2.   Travelling by bus.
3.   Shopping, including crowded stores.

Each of these modules is arranged into a hierarchy of 12 items. Only those
modules are used that are clinically relevant to the patient, so that any
particular patient might be treated with only one module, two, or all three.

Each hierarchy is graded in the usual way but is not based on the individual
needs of the patient; each patient has the same hierarchy. The individual
items refer to the environment of the unit and specify exactly the task to
be completed by the patient and the therapist, in order to reduce the risk
of misunderstanding.

The therapists used are members of staff who have had no training in behaviour
therapy. They are mostly student nurses doing a general training course, but
have also included medical students and enrolled nurses. The therapist is
provided with one page of explanation and instructions for the treatment
procedure and the patient is provided with a similar page. Both patient and
therapist have copies of the treatment modules.

As each item in the module is completed it is recorded on a record sheet
which is kept by the therapist and patient. The patient rates on a four point
scale the anxiety experienced whilst completing that item, each point on the
scale being precisely defined on the patient's instruction sheet. If the
patient rates the item as either '1' or '2' they proceed to the next item.
If they rate the item '3' then it must be repeated. A rating of '4' means
that the patient was unable to complete the task and they must then return
to the previous item. If a rating of '1' or '2' is not made after four
attempts at an item then the problem is referred back to the clinical psychologist for an analysis of the problem, but this has not yet been necessary.
The patient is expected to take considerable responsibility for his progress
through the treatment programme and is expected to attempt two items of
treatment each day. To complete the module the patient is required to repeat
the final item successfully three times, to provide a certain amount of
overlearning.

ASSESSMENT

An assessment of change is made on a nine point scale before the start of treatment and at the end. Ratings are made independently both by the patient and by a member of staff who is either the psychologist or psychiatrist. Ratings are made for both fear and for avoidance for each of the modules used in treatment. The behaviour chosen for rating is based on the final item in the module concerned.

We have not yet treated sufficient numbers of patients to come to any conclusion about the effectiveness of this treatment or whether improvement persists but the few patients treated to date have done extremely well. **Figs. 5.1 and 2** show an example of the pre and post treatment changes rated for fear and avoidance by one patient.

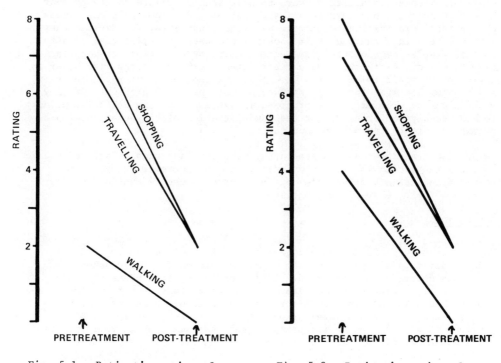

Fig. 5.1. Patient's rating of   Fig. 5.2. Patient's rating of
     fear (0–8 scale).   avoidance (0–8 scale).

We are planning to follow them up for at least six months after treatment is completed. The rating scale used is similar to the scales commonly used in other published research on the treatment of phobias so that the effectiveness of this treatment may be compared with other treatments used experimentally (Watson and Marks, 1971). No attempt has been made to provide another independent assessment as any independent rater would inevitably be aware of the treatment provided.

Comparison with desensitisation. The particular features of this treatment
compared with traditional desensitisation are:

1. The therapist receives a set of written instructions but
    no special training.
2. Responsibility for progress through the hierarchy rests
    with the untrained therapist and the patient.
3. Relaxation is not used in contiguity with the hierarchy.
4. The hierarchy is not designed individually for each patient.
5. Items within the hierarchy are not repeated until total
    extinction of anxiety is obtained.

Other aspects of treatment. The behavioural programme described forms the
central focus of treatment for these patients. However, other aspects of
management are not neglected. The family is usually seen by the medical
staff or psychiatric social worker, to help them to relate to the patient
as a 'coping' person rather than a sick person. Problems that may reduce
the patient's motivation to improve are also considered; for example they
may need help in arranging their housing, occupation or financial affairs.
In this respect we adopt the same eclectic and multidisciplinary approach
as with all our patients. The patient attends group meetings with other in
patients and staff twice a week when there is the opportunity to discuss
any problems related to the treatment, or more personal problems, if they
wish to do so. The patient's progress is discussed by the multidisciplinary
team at weekly conferences, but the administration of the behavioural programme is left to the patient and nurses.

Relaxation training sessions are part of the unit's programme and the phobic
patients can attend these if they wish to do so. However, they are not
required to attend and they are not instructed to use relaxation when carrying out their behavioural programme.

DISCUSSION

The treatment described can be regarded as a form of retraining which is
being applied to all patients with a primary diagnosis of agoraphobia who
have been severely incapacitated. It is applied by therapists who have
received only a single page of instructions which take less than five minutes to read. Whether the treatment will prove to be effective remains to
be seen, but will need a larger group of patients than has so far been
treated; it will depend on the standardised assessment which will include
a six month follow-up. If the treatment is successful it will not be
possible to say to what extent improvement is due to the behavioural programme and to what extent other aspects of in patient treatment have
contributed. However, this is an inherent problem in any treatment trial
involving in patients. There are many aspects of admission to hospital
which may have a therapeutic or non-therapeutic effect, and these are not
all immediately evident, not can they be adequately controlled for. The
assessment measures the total change occurring as a result of treatment,
and the behavioural programme is clearly only one aspect of this; but there
is no evidence to suggest that admission to hospital without specific treatment is useful in the management of agoraphobia, and we think that improvement should be attributed mainly to the behavioural programme.

So far as the behavioural aspect of treatment is concerned, several features should be mentioned. Relaxation has been omitted as there is now considerable evidence both from analogue and clinical studies that it makes little or no difference to desensitisation in phobic patients (Benjamin, Marks and Huson, 1972; Gillan and Rachman, 1974). Secondly, the absence of a hierarchy that is specific to the patient's needs can be justified by the evidence that alternative effective treatments such as implosion or modelling do not use a hierarchy at all and it has also been shown experimentally that the exact ordering of a hierarchy is not a prerequisite of successful treatment (Welch and Krapft, 1970). Effective treatments seem to share the main features of introducing the patients into the feared situation whilst preventing avoidance. We have retained a hierarchy because it does seem to be one effective way of achieving this. We have not attempted to repeat each item until anxiety is totally extinguished, but have aimed at reducing anxiety to levels at which it can be tolerated and avoidance does not occur. We think it may be important to teach the patient to tolerate a moderate degree of anxiety and to function in spite of it, as anxiety will centainly be encountered in the patient's subsequent experience. A treatment which involves coping only in the absence of anxiety might therefore lead to early relapse. For the same reason we have emphasized the need for the patient to share responsibility in carrying out treatment as this should make it easier for the patient to continue to take responsibility for his progress when at home.

Treatment is based on admission to hospital rather than within the community. There are probably advantages and disadvantages in either. In patient treatment the advantage is that we can observe the therapists closely in order to see the problems they encounter. We are able to control the environment in which treatment is being given, and the patient is away from influences at home which may reinforce the phobic behaviour.However there is also the problem that generalisation from hospital to home may not take place. The items in the modules have been made as detailed as possible to compensate for the therapists' lack of training, and we realise that such specific items might also prevent generalisation of the treatment effect. We have tried to prevent this by including different itineraries within each module. In addition, before the patient is discharged she goes home for at least one week-end in order to practice equivalent behaviour in the neighbourhood of her own home. Outpatient treatment might be used as a compromise but problems of travelling result in particular problems for agoraphobic patients, especially when residing in outlying districts.

So far we have found several practical difficulties encountered by the untrained therapists. For example they may rate the patient's anxiety themselves, rather than asking the patient to do so. They may fail to take appropriate action if the patient's rating shows a high degree of anxiety or inability to complete an item. At times they have simply forgotten to record the treatment given. However, these events have been uncommon and the therapists have usually welcomed the opportunity of sharing the responsibility for the patient's treatment.

This clinical treatment trial is at present in its early stages. If it proves to be successful then it might be adapted for use in mental hospitals and departments where skilled behaviour therapists are not yet available. It might also prove possible for the treatment to be provided in the community and by non-professionals, including members of the patient's family. We have limited the scope of this experimental treatment to agoraphobia and we would hesitate to suggest that such a treatment has value in the management of other conditions.

SUMMARY

Behaviour therapy for the treatment of agoraphobia appears to be effective but is not universally available. This deficit might be corrected by the use of unskilled therapists. A clinical trial is in progress which seeks to evaluate the efficacy of a behavioural programme for agoraphobia in patients which is administered by untrained nurse therapists.

REFERENCES

Agras, S., Sylvester, D. and Oliveau, D. (1969). The epidemiology of common fears and phobias. Comprehensive Psychiatry, 10, 151-156.

Benjamin, S., Marks, I.M., and Huson, J. (1972). Active muscular relaxation in desensitisation of phobic patients. Psychological Medicine 2, 381-390.

Gillan, P. and Rachman, S. (1974). An experimental investigation of desensitisation in phobic patients. British Journal of Psychiatry, 124, 392-401.

Marks, I.M. et al (1977). Clinical nurse specialists in psychiatry: A new source of therapists. British Journal of Psychiatry (in press).

Marks, I.M. and Herst, E.R., (1970). A survey of 1.200 agoraphobics in Britain. Social Psychiatry, 5, 16-24.

Watson, J. P. and Marks, I. M. (1971). Relevant and irrelevant in flooding a crossover study of phobic patients. Behaviour Therapy, 2, 275-293.

Welch, H.J. and Krapfl, J.E. (1970). Order of stimulus presentation in desensitisation. Paper presented at the 42nd Annual Meeting of the Midwestern Psychological Association, Cincinnati.

6. THE EFFECTS OF CAUSAL ATTRIBUTION AND COMBINED TREATMENT ON NEUROTIC ANXIETY

Wolfgang Tunner

Department of Clinical Psychology, University of Munich, W. Germany

INTRODUCTION

Usually patients with neurotic fears want to learn from their therapists whence come their disorders. Wanting to know the cause for symptoms which trouble one's life seems such a natural wish that its absence would be conspicuous.

Since behaviour therapy deals primarily with present conditions of anxiety, the above request of the patient is either not satisfied or only in a very inefficient and simple manner. At least two favourable consequences can be expected from a patients's "knowledge" of the individual origins of his anxiety:

1. A better understanding of the social function of anxiety and anxiety defence reactions in his existing situation and, consequently, a better understanding of the conditions of anxiety control.

2. A patient, expecting an explanation of the origins of his anxiety, will be more satisfied with the therapist if this expectancy is fulfilled. Presumably his motivation to cooperate in the therapeutic exercises will then be increased.

It could be objected that pointing out traumatic life conditions during childhood would encourage a patient to complain about fate rather than to participate in exercises appropriate to his present situation. Furthermore, it could be objected that the theoretical knowledge - even of general psychological points of view - does not permit the patient to be given an explanation, derived from his anamnestic data, with the degree of certainty he expects from his therapist.

It must be borne in mind that the lack of reliable explanation for the origins of the problem is not a sufficient reason to ignore its potential importance for treatment. What matters, therapeutically, is probably more the plausibility of the explanation than its scientific validity. We have gained the impression that it is usually sufficient to elaborate certain aspects of the causal relationships which are found with the help of the patient, regarding his individual past. Formulating general principles of conditioning, as is customary in behavioural therapy in order to make the origin of disorders understood, is often seen by the patient to be a means of simplifying matters and seems, if anything, to hinder cooperation in the therapeutic exercises.

A study was conducted in the Munich department with the main purpose of testing the assumption that attributing causes to neurotic fears lead to a favourable therapeutic effect.

Secondary aspects of this study included assumptions about the influence of the treatment of different indicators of anxiety. It was desired to develop the treatment in such a way that measures of anxiety, from the various reaction systems, would undergo a unidirectional positive change. Hodgson and Rachman (1974), surveying the literature of behaviour modification, suggested that concordance or synchronism among reactions is related to the intensity of the emotional arousal, the level of therapeutic demands, the treatment method, the specific indicators of anxiety that are assessed, and finally the time at which assessment takes place. Several hypotheses concerning synchronism of subjective, behavioural and autonomic variables are supported by results of these studies: the correlation depended on the therapeutic method (Tunner 1975) as well as on the choice of the autonomic variable. While heart rate always covaried with the subjective measure of anxiety, it did not covary with the GSR. In addition we observed that the physiological measure (GSR) changes gradually, in a positive direction, from the end of the treatment to the time of the follow-up (Oelkers and Tunner 1976).

From these considerations a number of hypotheses were formulated concerning the treatment of neurotic anxiety and a treatment program based on them was designed. It essentially draws on a combination of the principles of self-control, in-vivo-desensitization and rehearsal trials and, accordingly, consists of a) exercises for the self-perception of anxiety and anxiety defense reactions, b) analysis of the present function of anxiety, especially the social function, c) exercises in self-instruction and d) a number of rehearsal trials.

METHOD

Subjects

Twenty five patients, aged 21-55 years (mean:28), with specific phobias (claustrophobia, acrophobia, fear of darkness, etc.) and increased social anxiety were divided into three groups: two groups of 9 and a control group of 7 subjects.

Therapists

The therapists were 5 trained clinical psychologists, all of whom had at least 4 years of experience in behaviour therapy with neurotic patients. All subjects were seen by a series of therapists.

Assessment

The therapy outcome measure was the amount of anxiety, present immediately before and during a social stress situation, towards the specific phobic stimuli. Assessments of social anxiety were made before the beginning of treatment, after the 4th session, after the 8th session (end of therapy), and 6 weeks after the end of treatment. The measures taken were the systematic observation of behaviour, the recording of heart-rate and of spontaneous fluctuations of the GSR and, finally, the self-report ratings of actual anxiety. The fear of the specific phobic stimuli was assessed, before and after treatment, in the form of self-report ratings and a behavioural test whenever possible.

Treatment procedures and conditions

Treatment was administered im 8 sessions (2 group and 6 individual sessions). During the first session, a patient was told of the common elements under-lying anxiety states provoked by stimuli of different context (social or spe-cific phobic stimuli). This was achieved by pointing out the similarities in perceived physiological changes as in heart rate, palmar sweating, muscle tension and motor responses as well as in intended avoidance responses and reported feelings before the onset of either kind of stimuli. The patients were also made aware of the possibility of social reinforcements of their specific phobic symptoms. After this introduction and during the first ses-sion, relaxation training (Jacobson 1938) was carried out. All groups were instructed in relaxation training.

During the second session, systematic desensitization in-vivo was administered. Individualized phobic hierarchies with a number of items, ranging between 5 and 9, were used. Each subject was allowed to work through their hierarchy during the individual sessions (30 minutes each) and group sessions (90 minu-tes each). During the two group sessions a discussion of the desensitization procedure was carried out. The systematic desensitization was administered according to the method of Goldfried's (1973). Emphasis was placed on the development of self-control through self-instruction. In order to test the assumption about the effect of attributing causes to anxiety, conditions for the three groups were as follows:

Group 1: Nine subjects completed the standard treatment program and were also given a plausible explanation about the origins of their anxiety. The content of this explanation was derived from the subject's answers to a questionnaire. The questionnaire contained several sections pertaining to age and each pa-tient was requested to recollect situations in which he had experienced extre-me helplessness in connection with persons and/or objects. He was asked to describe the persons and situations connected with this helplessness. Later, the responses to the questionnaire were discussed with the patient, during which he was also asked to imagine the most distressing of the traumatic events and to describe it in detail. From these accounts and in conjunction with each patient some hypotheses were derived concerning the origins of his social and phobic anxiety. They were formulated in a way acceptable to the patient.

Group 2: Nine subjects completed the standard treatment program only.

Group 3: Seven subjects, as a control group, which went through the same pro-cedure of attribution as group 1 but did not complete the standard treatment program. Since the patients of all groups were supposed to have the same amount of contact with the therapists, the control group went also through a placebo procedure.

RESULTS AND DISCUSSION

Mean values of the measurements in the four assessment sessions i.e. before treatment, after fourth treatment session, after eighth treatment session and at the follow-up, were obtained for each group.

The changes in the different variables measured are illustrated in Fig. 6.1.

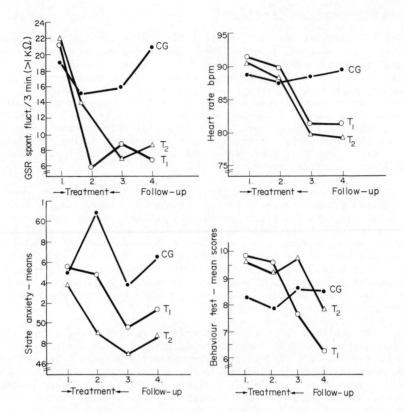

Fig. 6.1   The course of changes on GSR/spontaneous fluctuations/3mins
           (a), heart rate/bmp (b), state anxiety (c) and behavioural
           observation (d), before the beginning of treatment (1),
           after the 4th session (2), after the 8th session, end of
           treatment (3) and at 6 weeks' follow-up (4).
           T_1 = Standard treatment program and causal attribution;
           T_2 = Standard treatment program only;
           CG = Causal attribution only and placebo.

For statistical analyses, t-test on within-group and between group changes,
one way analyses of variance and tests for trend were employed. Results are
shown in Table 6.1. The statistical analyses revealed changes at 1% and 5%
levels and approaching a 10% level of significance. The results for the
control group, which had received attribution and a placebo procedure, were
far above the 10% level. Although our assessment of changes in anxiety levels,
in precence of specific phobic stimuli, was not as extensive as that carried
out in the case of social stimuli, i.e. no physiological measurements are
available in the former case, the pre- and post-treatment self-report ratings
and behavioural test used suggest that the decrease in anxiety, with the
presence of specific phobic stimuli, parallels that in the presence of social
anxiety provoking stimuli in the treated groups.

Table 6.1   Comparisons on the measured variables within groups and between groups.
T_1 = Standard treatment program and causal attribution
T_2 = Standard treatment program only
CG = Causal attribution only and placebo

* p = 0.10,   ** p = 0.05,   *** p = 0.01

Statistical Analyses	G S R Groups			Heart-rate Groups			Self-report rating Groups			Behaviour observation Groups		
	1	2	3	1	2	3	1	2	3	1	2	3
Trend (linear)	xx yes	xx yes	no	xx yes	xxx yes	no	no	xx yes	no	-	-	-
t-values (within groups)												
Before treatment - end of treatment	xx 2.52	xxx 4.74	-	x 2.17	xx 2.93	-	x 1.84	xx 2.67	-	xx 2.55	-	-
Before treatment - follow-up	xx 2.92	xx 3.16	-	-	xx 2.58	-	-	-	-	xx 2.80	x 2.05	-
t-values (between groups)												
End of treatment	x -1.90	xx -2.48										
Follow-up	xxx -5.52	xxx -3.14										

Fig. 6.2 shows the measures of anxiety for group 1 only, which received the standard treatment program as well as an interpretation about the causes of their anxiety.

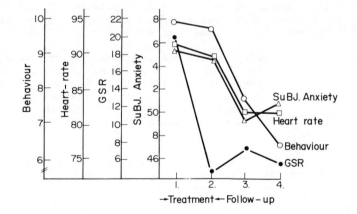

Fig. 6.2   The influence of treatment on different indicators of anxiety for treatment - group T_1 patients who received the standard treatment program as well as an interpretation about the causes of their anxiety. The representation makes it easy to detect the synchronism of the variables

Such representation makes it easy to detect the synchronism of the variables. It can be seen that the treatment had a unidirectional positive effect for all measures.

Worth mentioning are the results of a questionnaire asking the patients for a rating of treatment. The patients in all three groups stated that they were satisfied with treatment and that they considered the specific interventions useful for their daily lives. Only the subjects in the two groups, which went through the standard treatment program in order to overcome their anxiety, showed significant improvement. The control group showed no change in the stress situation, on autonomic, subjective and behavioural measures. The control group was, on the whole, most satisfied with the therapy, followed by group 1, which had received the standard treatment program and attribution. Group 2, having received the standard treatment program only, was generally the least satisfied. These results indicate that plausible explanations and friendly contact alone may ensure statements of satisfaction concerning therapy, but they are not guarantees for observable therapeutic success. The patients' satisfaction with the therapy is certainly a motivational prerequisite for the therapeutic exercises, but is not in itself a sufficient condition for a favourable treatment outcome.

A further aspect of evaluation was an analysis of patients' individual progressive course. This brought out some interesting points which led to several important hypotheses about prognosis for further studies and individual treatment in clinical practice. Schematically, we examined the direction of change in the several measures for each patient and found the following. Patients showing a change for the worse in the subjective measure, after 4 treatment sessions showed a deterioration or no change in the behavioural measure at the end of therapy compared with the assessment before treatment. This does not allow the reverse conclusion, that improvement on the subjective measure allows a prognosis about behavioural improvement at the end of therapy. From these individual observations, only the deterioration of the subjective measure furnishes a prognosis for the behavioural measure. In contrast, the deterioration of behaviour after four treatment sessions does not allow a prognosis about the subjective indicator of anxiety.

Further observations concerning concordance/discordance and synchronism/asynchronism will have to be studied systematically. These experiences support Hodgson's and Rachman's interest in investigating the influence of therapeutic methods on the various measures of anxiety. However, it seems that only if more is known about the individual differences of patients, and treatment is adjusted in accordance with these differences, will studies lead to results that can be generalized.

The effect of interpreting the origins of anxiety from the individual's life history will be further studied, though its effect seemed to be limited to satisfaction only with treatment in the present study.

SUMMARY

Based on the assumption that attributing causes to neurotic fears individually leads to a favourable therapeutic effect, 25 patients with specific phobias and increased social anxiety were divided into two groups of 9 and one group of 7 subjects. Group 1 completed a standard treatment program which consisted of exercises in self-analysis of anxiety and anxiety defense reactions, exercises in self-instructions and body relaxation, and a number of in-vivo rehearsal trials. Further, patients of this group were each given a plausible individual explanation about the origins of their social and phobic anxieties. The content of these explanations was taken from the subjects' answers on a questionnaire and from the anamnestic interview data. Group 2 completed the standard treatment program only. Patients of group 3 went through the same procedure of attribution as group 1, but did not complete the standard treatment. Statistical analysis revealed changes at 1% and 5% levels of significance and changes approaching significance at the 10% level for group 1 and group 2. The results for control group 3 were far above the 10% level. Nevertheless, group 3 was on the whole most satisfied with the therapy, followed by group 1 which had received the standard treatment program and attribution. Group 2 having received the standard treatment program only, was in general the least satisfied. Some hypotheses about the influence of treatment on different indicators of anxiety (synchronism) were discussed.

ACKNOWLEDGEMENTS

This study was supooreed by the "Deutsche Forschungs gemeinschoft" and the "Stiftung Volkswagen Werk". The author wishes to express his gratitude to Karin Munzel and Heinz Kolbe, whose help made the completion of the present work possible.

REFERENCES

Goldfried M.R. (1973). Reduction of generalized anxiety through a variant of systematic desensitisation. In M.R. Goldried and M. Merbaum (Eds.) Behavior change through self-control. Holt, New York.

Hodgson, R., and Rachman S. (1974). Desynchrony in measures of fear. Behavior Research and Therapy, 12, 319-326.

Jacobson, E. (1938). Progressive relaxation, Chicago, University of Chicago Press.

Oelkers, C. and Tunner, W. Experimentelle Untersuchung zur Angstbehandlung durch Selbstergulation. Zeitschrift fur Klinische Psychologie und Psychotherapie, (in press).

Tunner, W. (1975). Systematische Desensibilisierung und das Lernen von Strategien zur Bewaltigugg von Angst. In: I. Florin and W. Tunner (Eds.) Therapie der Angst. Munchen, Urban und Schwarzenberg, 221-239.

7. BEHAVIOURAL RESEARCH INTO OBSESSIVE NEUROSIS

Richard Stern

Institute of Psychiatry, London

Obsessional illness presents a difficult therapeutic problem. Often patients are severely incapacitated by rituals which take over their life to such an extent that it seems impossible to understand the illness. At the other extreme mild rituals such as those so common in children are considered normal. However, it is patients with severe rituals which they cannot control and which they find extremely incapacitating that are the subject of this presentation. I intend to review recent work in this area carried out largely at the Maudsley Hospital. Then some case illustrations will be reviewed to show just how the treatment is carried out. Finally, I shall indicate some directions of on going research.

In 1971 Levy and Meyer reported an uncontrolled study in which patient's rituals were totally restricted. This involved continual supervision during the waking hours by nurses who were instructed to prevent the patient carrying out any rituals. This supervision was carried out for between 1 and 4 weeks during which the patient was gradually exposed to situations which evoked rituals and again prevented from carrying those out. At follow-up which varied from between 1 to 6 years, 6 out of the 8 patients treated were either much improved or symptom free and the remaining 2 were 70% improved on the ratings used. The authors speculated about the mechanism of improvement. They called the treatment "response prevention" and likened it to Baum's work (1970) on fixated responses in rats. In addition, they considered that modelling and flooding may have been important aspects.

The relative importance of modelling and flooding was further examined in a study of 10 patients by Rachman, Hodgson and Marks (1971). All patients were treated in hospital, and in the first three weeks had fifteen sessions of control treatment (relaxation). Over the second three weeks patients were assigned at random to fifteen sessions either of modelling or of flooding. Flooding consisted of encouraging patients to make contact with an object which they feared was contaminated. During modelling each step was first demonstrated to the patient by a calm and reassuring therapist and the patient then "shadowed" his therapist's actions. All measures showed improvement after flooding and modelling, both of which were significantly superior to the relaxation control treatment. Flooding and modelling did not differ significantly from each other. The authors suggest that this could be because both treatments act through a common factor which might also be present in Levy and Meyer's (1971) technique. What all three techniques have in common is exposure to the situation which causes discomfort, along with tacit prevention of rituals in each case. Treatment was effective despite the lack of twenty-four hour supervision which Meyer deemed important, but treatment was more extensive in the sense that it was carried on in the patient's own home in some cases after hospital treatment had been completed.

In a later paper, the same authors gave a further five patients modelling plus flooding (Hodgson, Rachman and Marks, 1972). This was slightly superior to either modelling or flooding alone, on a few measures. Improvement continued to six month follow up on these patients, and the others previously treated by flooding or modelling alone. A possible implication is that flooding and modelling in some way facilitate each other, and that modelling allowed more successful exposure, and hence the combination of treatments becomes more effective. This is not surprising when comparing the effectiveness of modelling in treatment of phobic disorders as demonstrated by Bandura (1969).

There still remain unanswered questions about the role of response-prevention: is exposure to the contaminant the important factor, or is it interruption of the avoidance response?

Boulougouris and Bassiakos (1973), reported a marked reduction in chronic obsessional symptoms following a treatment called "prolonged flooding". Three patients were exposed in the presence of the therapist to in-vivo situations which triggered off discomfort and were not allowed to perform their rituals after touching contaminated objects. They were also flooded in fantasy with images of contaminating objects. The mean total therapy was 22 hours. There was no attempt to assess the separate effects of supervised contamination and ritual prevention and there was no baseline period of observation since the first rating was made immediately before beginning the first treatment.

Mills and his associates (1971), compared the effect in two patients of forced exposure to objects which provoked rituals, without response prevention, with the effect of exposure combined with ritual prevention. In this study an objective measure of ritual behaviour was used: when the patient approached a washbasin a cumulative recorder was automatically activated, indicating the frequency and duration of handwashing during exposure alone, but a significant and lasting reduction in compulsive behaviour occurred after the introduction of ritual prevention into the treatment procedure. In a further study (Mills et al 1973), the same group compared the effects of giving verbal instructions with exposure and with ritual-prevention in a series of five patients with rituals. They concluded that ritual prevention following exposure was a necessary condition for the elimination of rituals.

Exposure to contaminated objects before prevention of rituals produced either no change or even an increase in rituals, and the authors propose that exposure during and after prevention of the ritual may interact with the effect of ritual prevention to eliminate handwashing.

However, this study had serious faults. Control exposure periods were not of comparable length to ritual prevention periods, and only 3 our of 5 patients with washing rituals actually had a period of exposure without ritual prevention. The duration of exposure ranged from 7 to 40 days while the period of ritual prevention ranged from 10 to 14 days.

An attempt to overcome these faults and to further demonstrate the importance of the components of response prevention was made by Lipsedge (1974). In this pilot study there were three treatment conditions. The first was response prevention in which the patient was encouraged to handle the objects most likely to cause handwashing, and then gently but firmly prevented from washing. The second was called "undoing the undoing" after Freud's description

of obsessional rituals as "Ungeschehenmachen" which literally means "making
unhappen" but which the Editor of the Standard Edition translates as "Undoing
what has been done" (Freud, 1959). Here the patient was encouraged to alter-
nately handle the "contaminated object" for a minute then to wash for a minute. The total amount of time spent, and the timing of the measures was the
same as in the response prevention condition. The third condition was called
"washing". Here the patient had to wash his hands repeatedly for three one
hour periods, separated by an hour's interval.

The first of these treatments (response prevention) consisted of exposure,
the second (undoing the undoing) involved exposure plus washing rituals, and
the third entailed washing alone. The results showed "undoing" to be consistently superior to "washing" which supports the view that exposure is an
important factor. In addition there were many significant improvements in
favour of "response prevention" compared with "washing", also pointing towards
the therapeutic effect of exposure. Unfortunately, this study also had its
faults. Of the 12 patients treated only 7 completed the second phase of the
crossover design and only two completed the third phase, hence there was a
lack of balance in the allocation of treatments. There were also serious
problems in measurement which are common to much work in the area. Nevertheless, this work was important in suggesting that continuous supervision
following exposure is necessary, and it paved the way for larger studies where
the emphasis was shifted to an examination of the relationship between exposure and modelling.

Following reports of short term improvement after behavioural treatments,
Marks, Hodgson and Rachman (1975), reported the results over two years follow
up of twenty patients with chronic obsessive compulsive neurosis who were
treated by real life (in-vivo) exposure (alone or with modelling) in a partially controlled design (Rachman et al 1971; Hodgson et al, 1972). The follow-up
showed improvement to be maintained during the two years after discharge. In
this study, exposure was given in three possible ways. In five patients
exposure was slow up a hierarchy with the therapist modelling each action.
In another group of five patients, exposure was rapid near the top of the
hierarchy without prior modelling by the therapist of the required actions.
In a third group, ten patients had rapid exposure plus modelling.

When certain patients made repeated requests for reassurance about possible
disastrous consequences, these were regarded as compulsive rituals and specific reassurance was not given. Even the patient's relations and friends
were advised to refuse requests for reassurance about possible effects of not
carrying out the ritual, and told to reply to the patient "I am afraid I cannot answer that sort of question".

The results of that study showed there was no significant improvement after
three weeks of relaxation, but improvement occurred within the first three
weeks of treatment by real life exposure. This was significantly greater
than after relaxation, and the gain continued until six months follow-up.

Treatment by real-life exposure with self imposed response prevention effectively reduced rituals in two thirds of the chronic obsessional patients.
Treatment was short (three to eight weeks) and did not involve continual supervision. All eight patients who were much improved after three weeks exposure
treatment remained so at two year follow-up, as did all twelve patients who
were much improved at six months follow-up. The improvement never began after

relaxation treatment, but only with exposure treatment. The study indicated also that those patients who were able to reduce the rituals between sessions during the first few days of treatment, did very well by the end of therapy. There was no significant difference between the patients who were exposed either rapidly or slowly with modelling. We now use rapid exposure where possible, but the rate of exposure is, of course, often governed by the patient.

Perhaps the details of therapeutic problems are best illustrated by turning from the date of controlled studies and providing some case illustrations;

A thirty year old housewife had rituals involving checking bills, receipts and money, door locks, gas taps, electrical and car switches and household rubbish prior to throwing it away. As a result of hoarding, she had 300 newspapers on a sideboard and one room of the house completely filled with undisposed rubbish. Washing of her hands or clothes took four or more times than the average person. In the year prior to her referral, her rituals had seriously increased, sleep was reduced, her sexual and marital relationships deteriorated and her eldest child began to show abnormal behaviour.

The two main target problems were "shopping without checking money or shopping list" and "disposing of rubbish without checking contents". These targets were rated 6 and 8 by the patient on an 0-8 scale, where 8 indicated maximum pathology. The first obsession occupied 1-2 hours per day and the second about 1 hour daily.

Adequate treatment required inpatient admission for six weeks. Initially, the patient was supervised during shopping, and dissuaded from using her shopping list. The amount of change in her purse was altered so that she could not recheck it, and she was asked to reduce the time she spent choosing each item. Rituals decreased despite resistance from the patient. Treatment next concerned cleansing rituals concerning the patient's nine months old infant. She was dissuaded from sterilising facecloths and flannels after each use, and dust from the vacuum cleaner was spread around her room. Further written instructions were provided for the ward nursing staff to continue treatment between sessions. The patient was resistant and critical of treatment, but the therapist persisted and the rituals diminished markedly.

Because the husband had been involved in the patient's rituals a conjoint interview was arranged with the patient, her husband and the therapist. The husband agreed to co-operate in preventing several of his wife's obsessive rituals. The marital relationship presents further problems. The patient constantly belittled her husband while he teased his wife that his job and their money were insecure; this increased her checking and other rituals. In early marital interviews, the couple's attention was therefore drawn to this and both made 'contracts' to change this behaviour. Prior to discharge from hospital, the patient was accompanied home by the therapist and further prevention of checking rituals was carried out in her car and at home. After the patient had driven the car, the therapist instructed her to stop and leave the car without checking, and in the knowledge that the therapist might alter some of the switches. The patient's need to check the car rapidly diminished. The same applied to the patient's difficulties with letter writing. She was asked to write several letters without checking spelling and punctuation, and to post these immediately.

Despite the complications and initial gloomy prognosis, the patient made remarkable improvement. By discharge she had improved to the point where she only made a check of car switches. Checking of dials on the cooker and the back door, and other checks, were eliminated. The couple spoke more positively to one another and made decisions more democratically. At discharge, the target problems were rated as 1 and 2 respectively, and neither obsession occupied more than five minutes per day.

Treatment had been spread over 25 sessions during five months, six weeks of which were as an inpatient together with the younger child. Treatment occupied 39 hours by the therapist, plus 6 hours of contract marital therapy.

This case shows how target problems can be arrived at despite the confusion at first sight. Obsessional patients often present a range of symptomatology and the therapist may be puzzled about where to begin. As in this case, the aim is to commence with a simple item ("not checking the shopping list"), until this was mastered. Then a more difficult item was tackled, until gradually less symptoms were present. It then became clear that the husband's involvement had to be dealt with before further progress could be made, and so this was commenced at the appropriate point. The same case also demonstrates a common relationship between depression and obsessional illness. Often when a patient becomes depressed there is an increase in the obsessive-compulsive features. Sometimes the depression requires treatment in its own right, e.g. by tricyclic anti-depressant medication, and this may be a necessary step before behavioural treatment can be effective.

In some cases there is no avoidance behaviour as in the first case illustration, nor is the main problem one of checking an activity. The main compulsive action may be a cleaning ritual as in the case of a 29 year old housewife who spent so much time cleaning her house that she had no time left to play with her two children or engage in leisure pursuits. This was despite the fact that she was an intelligent woman with a degree in modern languages. She described feeling extremely anxious before carrying out the cleaning, and was very tense during this activity. When she had cleaned the whole house to her satisfaction, she felt a sense of relief. Compulsive rituals often serve to reduce discomfort in this way as demonstrated by Roper, Rachman and Hodgson (1973). Although she made a moderate effort herself to resist this excessive cleaning, she considered it sensible to engage in the activity, despite the fact that the new wallpaper was worn away with excessive dusting and all her housecleaning left no time for other pursuits. There was no avoidance of dirt per se in her case, as she could plunge her arms into a dustbin without anxiety. She did not mind spreading dust around her house as long as she was allowed to clean it up afterwards, and all her rituals were centered in the house alone.

Treatment of this patient clearly had to be carried out in the patient's own home as all her rituals occurred there. This is often necessary, as suggested by Rachman et al (1973). In view of the fact that her tension and anxiety decreased after the performance of a cleaning ritual, it was decided to set goals of limited cleaning with an agreed upon time before allowing her to complete the cleaning procedure, e.g. the therapist visited her house and watched her going through an elaborate window cleaning procedure in her kitchen. The therapist suggested that she did not clean half the kitchen window (which was conveniently divided into two sections) until his visit to the house next

week. The patient would not agree to this at first, stating that she thought
she would not be able to overcome the urge to clean the entire window. She
stated "once the cleaning gets going, I just cannot stop". The therapist
decided to help with this in two ways: firstly, he marked the window that
was to be left unclean by attaching adhesive tape to the relevant panes,
and furthermore, said that if she felt the overwhelming desire to clean
before his next visit, she had to telephone him first "to ask permission".
In this way, the patient managed to leave half the window uncleaned for one
week for which she was heavily praised by the therapist and her husband.
Subsequently, similar procedures were applied until she could leave the
whole window, and also keep down her dusting activities elsewhere to reasonable limited.

During the home treatment sessions an enormous cupboard full of cleaning materials, detergents, polishes and cleansing fluids was discovered. As part of
treatment, the patient agreed not to replenish these stocks until there was
only one container of each type left in the cupboard. Moreover, she was to
save the money that she would normally have spent in this manner, and spend
it instead on buying something for herself e.g. flowers or make-up.

Along with the cleaning rituals, this patient had an overwhelming urge to be
meticulous about everything. For instance, in the bathroom a shelf of lotions,
powders and tooth cleaning materials were always laid out in an orderly manner.
The therapist modelled disorderlies for her by squeezing some toothpaste
around the sink, leaving the cap off the tube, writing on the mirror with
soap and rearranging the lotions. The patient had no problems following suit,
but stated that she could not leave the bathroom like this for long after the
therapist's departure, She was asked to leave as much "disorderliness" as
possible for as long as possible until the therapist's visit next week. The
only item she succeeded in leaving was the writing on the bathroom mirror:
the rest was restored to its previous pristine state one hour after the therapist left the home. As before, this problem was tackled by breaking it down
to small items, e.g. toothpaste cap to be left off. When she succeeded at
this for one week, another item was added until she became less meticulous
and her cleaning activities came under control.

These two case illustrations clearly show how rituals may take different
behavioural forms. In the first illustration checking rituals predominated,
in the second the main ritual involved cleaning. In order to examine the
behavioural forms that rituals can take, a study is underway to quantify
this along with other phenomenological aspects of obsessional illness.

The main kinds of behaviour that are observed in patients with obsessional
rituals can be arbitrarily divided into the following forms:

        1.   Repeating
        2.   Checking
        3.   Cleaning
        4.   Avoiding
        5.   Slowing
        6.   Striving for completeness
        7.   Being meticulous

Most of the descriptions of behavioural form are self-explanatory. "Slowness"

presents a special problem, and may require illustration. Such a patient
might take one hour to shave, the whole ritual being frustrated by numerous
slow repetitive circular movements of his electric shaver. The same patient
when cleaning his teeth needed 192 slow meticulous brush strokes for each
application of toothpaste and for each rinse, the whole ritual taking about
half an hour.

In his work on the problems of obsessional illness, Lewis, (1936), stated that
resistance against the obsession with recognition that this resistance came
from the patient's own free will, was the hallmark of obsessional illnesses.
This could be useful in separating obsessional ideas from psychotic ones,
but often when there is a clear history of rituals and ruminations, the presence of resistance cannot always be elicited. Leaving this aside, it is
apparent that response-prevention interferes with the patient's free-will.
It imposes an external resistance against the performance of rituals. This
can be seen as making the ineffectual internal personal resistance of the
patient into an effective external resistance controlled at first by the
therapist, which the patient then models himself on (or identifies himself
with, to use another terminology). As a result of behavioural treatment,
many patients have successfully come to resist impulses to perform rituals
whereas previously they were unsuccessful.

A further aspect being looked into is the relationship of anxiety or other
strong emotion to the ritual. Here one hypothesis might be that the ritual
serves an anxiety reducing function, and this would tend to reinforce its
occurrence. Roper et al (1973) conducted an experiment to determine whether
the execution of a potentially "harmful" act produced discomfort, and whether
the act of checking produced relief. They noted a difference between those
patients whose rituals involved mainly "checking" and those whose main problem was "washing". A checking ritual was found to reduce discomfort in
most subjects but in a minority of "checkers" the discomfort was actually
increased by the ritual (but never in the "washers"). Current research at
the Maudsley is looking into this apparent paradox in a large series of
patients. The same study hopes to examine the common clinical experience
that a patient will state that he feels his rituals are completely absurd,
but nevertheless feels compelled to carry them out.

Another area of interest is the effect that a responsible other person might
have on the occurrence of rituals. In therapy it sometimes happens that a
patient will agree to stop ritualising if the therapist himself agrees to
take responsibility for whatever might occur as a result of the ritual not
being completed.

In addition, some patients' rituals are "situation bound" e.g. they occur
only in their own home and nowhere else. On the other hand, most of the
sample tested so far had rituals which occurred anywhere they happened to
be. Another relevant question concerns family involvement in the ritual.
This is clearly very important in some cases as shown by the case illustrations.

The first case illustration demonstrates the well known relationship between
depression and obsessional illness. Would treatment with an anti-depressant
drug reduce the severity of obsessional rituals? Would an anti-depressant
drug act synergistically with exposure therapy to reduce obsessional rituals?

Answers to these, and other questions may come from an ongoing controlled trial of clomipramine ("Anafranil"), with exposure plus modelling. In this study patients are randomly allocated to drug or placebo medication, and further randomly allocated to three weeks exposure plus modelling versus six weeks of the same procedure. In this way we hope to elucidate the optimum duration of time to continue treatment. It is theoretically and practically important to find out whether a long duration of treatment prevents relapse in the future more effectively than a shorter "dose". Of further theoretical interest is the possible mechanism of action of tricyclic drugs in obesssional disorders: are the patients so treated cured of a clinical or subclinical depressive illness which somehow reduces the ritualistic behaviour, or does the drug increase drive level in some non-specific way? To attempt to answer these and other questions raised in this chapter a large number of measures inuluding those of depression will be undertaken in the study referred to. The collection and analysis of the data relevant to the questions raised here may take several years. The answers will probably have to wait until then.

SUMMARY

The literature concerning behavioural treatments of obsessive compulsive neurosis is reviewed critically in order to examine such theoretical issues as the role of response prevention in treatment. Some case illustrations are given to illuminate these issues. Some on-going research is briefly described to show the direction of the current of new ideas in the area.

REFERENCES

Bandura, A. (1969). Principles of Behaviour Modification. Holt, Reinhart and Winston, New York.

Baum, M. (1970). Extinction of avoidance responding through response prevention (flooding). Psychological Bulletin, 74, 274-284.

Boulougouris, J.C., and Bassiakos, L. (1973). Prolonged flooding in fantasy with obsessive compulsive neurosis. Behaviour Research and Therapy, 11, 227-231.

Freud, S. (1959). Inhibitions, Symptoms and Anxiety (1926). Standard Ed. Vo. 20, London, Hogarth.

Hodgson, R. Rachman, S. and Marks, I.M. (1972). The treatment of obsessive-compulsive neurosis: follow up and further findings. Behaviour Research and Therapy, 10, 181-189.

Levy, R. and Meyer, V. (1971). Ritual prevention in obsessional patients. Proceedings of Royal Society of Medicine, 64, 115-120.

Lewis, A. (1936). Problems of obsessional illness. Proceedings of Royal Society of Medicine, 29, 325-336.

Lipsedge, M.S. (1974). Therapeutic approaches to compulsive rituals: a pilot study. M. Phil. dissertation, University of London.

Marks, I.M., Hodgson, R. and Rachman, S. (1975). Treatment of chronic obsessive neurosis by in-vivo exposure. British Journal of Psychiatry, 177, 349-364.

Mills, H. L., Agras, W.S., Barlow, D.W. and Mill, J.R. (1973). Compulsive rituals treated by resposse prevention. Archives General Psychiatry, 28, 524-529.

Mills, H.L., Barlow, D.H., and Bauch, J. (1971). Paper to Association of Advancement of Behaviour Therapy. Washington.

Rachman, S. Hodgson, R. and Marks, I.M. (1971). Treatment of chronic obsessive-compulsive neurosis. Behaviour Research and Therapy. 9, 237-247.

Rachman, S., Marks, I.M. and Hodgson, R. (1973). The treatment of obsessive-compulsive neurotics by modelling and flooding in-vivo. Behaviour Research and Therapy, 11, 463-471.

Roper, G., Rachman, S., and Hodgson, R. (1973). An experiment on obsessional checking. Behaviour Research and Therapy. 11, 271-277.

8. THE ROLE OF THE PATIENT IN MODELLING/FLOODING TREATMENT

Gisela Roper

Institute of Psychology, University of Munich, W. Germany

This paper discusses some side-issues in the use of modelling and flooding treatments, for obsessive compulsive neurotics, which are rarely mentioned in detail in the literature but which are of considerable importance for the overall outcome of treatment. The viewpoints presented are based on 4 years of clinical experience in applying modelling/flooding treatments to obsessive compulsive patients at the Maudsley Hospital in London. During that period 35 to 40 obsessional patients were treated 15 within my own research project (Roper, Rachman and Marks 1975).

This work with obsessive-compulsive neurotics was influenced by my colleagues Drs. S. Rachman, I. Marks and R. Hodgson to whom I am greatly indebted. The opinions discussed below were developed either through working with them as therapists, or in discussions with them on treatment programmes or on the handling of a patient. The aspects of treatment, discussed in this paper, will be familiar to those experienced in modelling/flooding treatments for obsessive-compulsive neurotics, but varying opinions have been expressed on these aspects and a discussion of some of the points is long overdue. For those therapists who have not applied such treatment approaches to obsessional patients a discussion of some practical clinical considerations could also be of value.

The main point under discussion is the extent to which an obsessional patient should be involved in planning and conducting his own treatment programme. This theme will be developed in relation to:

1. The description of the treatment given to a patient.
2. The treatment rationale.
3. A patient's voluntary confrontation with feared situations.
4. A patient's decision to accept treatment.
5. An assessment of motivation.
6. Family-involvement in therapy.
7. Arrangement of response prevention.
8. After-treatment care.

1. While the role of a patient is seen as that of an active participant in the treatment programme, the function of the therapist is considered largely as that of a supportive adviser and supervisor. The therapist's aim is to equip a patient with appropriate skills which the latter can himself apply to an ever increasing extent.

After an extensive behavioural interview, a patient is always given a detailed description of the treatment proposed. He must be given a clear idea of what is going to happen during the treatment. This includes informing him of the possibility of choosing either a graded or a rapid approach, so that he can decide for himself which treatment he would prefer. However, the patient is always advised to to which type of treatment would be most suitable for him, graded or rapid type of exposure, after gaining a clinical impression of the severity of his disorder his motivation for change, his trust in the type of treatment involved and his general anxiety.

If it is suggested for the patient to participate in a research project, the treatment plan is explained. He is also told that he is entitled to refuse participation and to ask for a slower or faster treatment.

2.   The description of the treatment proposed is followed by a presentation of the treatment-rationale. A brief and simply formulated outline of aspects, such as the development and maintenance of obsessive-compulsive symptoms, is given to him. The learning principles, which form the theoretical background of modelling/flooding treatment approaches, are also explained. The patient's comprehension of the treatment rationale is of great importance, if he is expected to take an active part in treatment.

As an unsystematic observation it is found that a patient's understanding of the treatment rationale is a useful indication of the extent of the co-operation to be expected and thus, indirectly of the treatment outcome.

3.   A patient is always promised that he will not be forced into a feared situation. At no point will a new treatment step be introduced unexpectedly without his permission. Some therapists disagree with this point. Boulougouris and Bassiakos (1973) reported that a patient's reluctance to enter a feared situation could be overcome by firm persuasion. They reported two incidences of strong fear reactions in such situations where the patients spontaneously described a situation which they considered of crucial importance in the onset of their illness. However, it is thought, apart from the ethical questions involved, strong pressure could well, in some cases, have an antitherapeutic effect. A patient might not experience a feeling of achievement after such a session and conclude that he has performed the approach behaviour only under the therapist's pressure. This would considerably diminish the learning effect.

Also, an anticipatory anxiety about the next treatment session might lead to a decision to discontinue treatment. However, at various points in most treatments, the therapist must talk a patient into confronting the next situation by convincing him of the necessity for this step.

4.   Before discussing with a patient whether or not he will accept treatment, stress must be laid on the demands that the treatment will make on his willingness to co-operate and therefore on his desire for change. It is also pointed out that, on the basis of the therapists support and expert advice, the treatment is fundamentally different from attempts to overcome such fears without professional help. Personally, a patient's decision to accept the approach offered is never accepted immediately after the description of the treatment and the presentation of its rationale. Instead, a letter or a phone-call a week or so later is requested so as to give him the chance to consider all the details of the information supplied.

5.   The most difficult part of the pre-treatment assessment is the estimation of the motivation for change. There are obviously certain questions the

therapist tries to clarify, such as whether a patient comes of his own voli-
tion or has he been sent by his family? There is also the evaluation of
the usual psychiatric prognostic factors like maintenance of interests or a
job, good family or social relationships, etc. (Meyer-Gross, Slater and Roth
1969). As mentioned earlier, a patient's interest is understanding the
treatment rationale can give an additional useful hint for assessing his
motivation. Also an exposure task of moderate difficulty could be given and
the patient's response closely observed. Refusal to carry out the task would
cast some doubt on his cooperation later in treatment. However, it is early
to say, which factors have positive prognostic properties in such patients
treated with flooding and/or modelling therapy.

6.   When a patient has accepted treatment, the choice between hospital or
home-treatment is usually self indicative, as for example, when the main
problems are centered around the home-situation. Of course this has to be
discussed in detail with a patient.

Closely related to the place of treatment is the extent of family involvement
in the therapy. A good deal of family or partner participation, during
treatment mainly in the case of home treatment and especially after its termination, is of great importance for the overall treatment outcome and the
maintenance of improvement. However patients without a family or a partner
also respond satisfactorily to this type of treatment. If the treatment is
conducted in a patient's home, other family members must be informed about
the significance of requests for reassurance. As observed during previous
research by Rachman, Hodgson and Marzillier(1970) and Rachman, Hodgson and
Marks (1971) many patients, when instructed to refrain from rituals, tended
to ask for reassurance ("Is it alright to touch the floor and not to wash
hands afterwards?" or "Do you think, I might have put some glass in the
cake?").   For many patients, reassurance by other people seems to serve a
comparable function to the actual performance of a ritual. This of course
has to be explained to a patient in the first place. Giving an explanation
to family members, together with the instruction not to give reassurance,
usually proves insufficient. Role-playing sessions are recommended, where
the client asks questions for reassurance and a family member answers in
stereotyped phrases such as "I am sorry, I cannot answer that sort of question".
Such stereotyped answers appear to be far more effective than long discussions.
It is also worth using different examples in the sessions because obsessionals tend to ask particularly shrewd questions which are not easily detected
as questions for reassurance.

In some cases it is also useful to devise a contract, which can be written
if preferred between a patient and other family-members, the therapist and
a patient or the therapist and a family member. It is sometimes necessary
to establish, and maintain by contract, the support and positive reinforcement
of a family member during treatment.

For example, if a female patient completed a certain number of treatment
assignments, her husband would give her a little present or take her out for
dinner. Or, if the husband took at least 15 minutes to ask about the day's
treatment programme, the patient would have to tackle one further task.

Apart from demanding a partner's or family's co-operation, it should be stressed to them that a patient is responsible for the proper execusion of his own

treatment programme.

This is to prevent family-members from rushing after a patient continually to watch over his progress. This is particularly important after a course of hospital treatment, as many patients report constant attempts by family-members to supervise whether or not they resume their ritualistic activities. These attempts are often interpreted, by a patient, as founded on mistrust of their improvement and of their newly learned skills.

In some cases it becomes obvious to the therapist and the family-members, that a pattern has developed of a family either participating in the ritualistic activities of ,a patient or protecting him from any ritual or fear-provoking situation. Such patterns not infrequently become so deeply engrained that their alteration would necessitate an extensive therapeutic intervention.

In such cases where a patient has been prevented from leaving home mainly by his obsessional problems and indeed wishes to live independently away from his family, then a training in basic skills of how to look after his own daily needs may be advisable instead of training sessions within a family setting. Obviously, such major steps as altering a patient's life situation can not be introduced by the therapist against a patient's will. However, he might well be in need of support from the therapist to build up some confidence in his own abilities to look after himself.

Family-involvement, not directly related to the treatment itself, is important when assessing the effect of a positive treatment outcome on the family structure or partnership. Such possible effects need to be discussed adequately in a family conference especially if a client is very dependent on his partner, or the symptoms have been the main topics of discussion for many years. Additional marriage counselling for non-compulsive aspects of marital problems is also advised by some therapists.

To return to the course of modelling/flooding treatment, one always tries to involve a patient as early as possible in the planning of the treatment-programme, including treatment-sessions and between-treatment tasks. Whether it is a course of hospital treatment or home treatment, between session assignments are planned with a patient. At the beginning of each session the degree of success with the assignments is discussed.

7.   This approach of response prevention under self-control is at variance with Meyer and Chesser (1970) who claim that 24 hour supervision of response prevention is essential for a positive treatment-outcome. Six years of experience with flooding treatment, without supervised response prevention, have shown that it is nevertheless effective. However it is possible that 24 hour supervision may be essential in some cases.

There are a number of reasons why response prevention under self-control could be a more favourable approach. Firstly in most institutions it would be impossible to provide the necessary amount of nursing-staff time. Secondly, continuous supervision would certainly counteract the patient's active participation in the treatment and delay him in adopting the principles of treatment and in regaining confidence that he is able to cope with fear-provoking situations and urges to ritualise. It is thought that the initial enthusiasm of a motivated patient is wasted in a fully supervised response-prevention programme. At termination of a treatment, the difficulties that patients encounter as the therapist fades out of a treatment process could be unnecessarily increased.

In a recent 24-hour response prevention programme with two obsessionals (one with checking and one with obsessional slowness problems), both patients soon reported negative feelings about being followed around and being given instructions continuously. Naturally the nursing-staff found it very strenuous constantly to observe the patient and give instructions. They also reported negative feelings towards a patient, usually due to the latter's reluctance to cooperate.

8.   At termination of a treatment proper, the likelihood of recurring fears should be pointed out to a patient. With the skills with which he has learned to counteract irrational fears, he should be able to cope with most recurrences. It is strongly advised that a patient should come back for a booster-treatment-session if he has ritualised again or avoided one of the old feared situations.

At this stage the amount of former active participation will pay off. In addition, without the background of some knowledge of learning principles of this treatment, a patient would be less likely to recognize 'hesitating to enter certain situations' as danger signals, or voluntarily to recontaminate himself or to untidy his personal belongings without the therapist's repeated instructions.

During the after-care phase it is recommended that even much-improved patients should be seen on several occasions (probably twice at fortnightly and twice at monthly intervals) in order to discuss further plans for their future and possible instances of old fears.

The possibility of establishing obsessional ex-patients-family-groups should also be mentioned. Several of these have been run by Dr. I. Marks (1975) and his nurse-therapist team at the Maudsley Hospital in London. It proved extremely helpful to many patients and their families to discuss problems and their solution after completion of a course of treatment. The problems discussed were, for example, support to be given by the family, how to handle set-backs in progress, etc.   Sometimes contracts were suggested by fellow-patients or other group members. Many patients reported that these groups provided a new incentive to carry on the struggle fully to overcome their fears.

In this paper the view was stressed that a patient should be encouraged as much as possible actively to participate in his own treatment. It was suggested that the patient should be given a detailed description of his treatment, as well as a simply formulated account of its theoretical background. The active role of a patient in therapy was also discussed in the context of voluntary confrontation with feared situations, a patient's decision to accept treatment, the assessment of his motivation, the involvement of a patient's family in treatment, the arrangement of response prevention programmes and the problems of after-care.

It is stressed that this is a presentation of personal clinical views, most of which have not been objectively evaluated. Some of the issues discussed could well be investigated in more detail. For example, the importance of a patient's understanding of the theoretical background of the treatment, the fostering of support by family members through role-playing-sessions and/or contracts, the necessity of treatment assignments between treatment sessions and the necessity of after-care following a successful treatment termination, could all be evaluated by controlled experimental research.

Now that the general efficiency of the treatment has been established, and some of the major therapeutic elements have been isolated, one should attempt to maximize the efficacy of the total treatment packages. Therefore careful investigation of the kind of factors that have been mentioned becomes of increasing importance.

SUMMARY

Some clinical side issues of modelling/flooding treatment for obsessive compulsive neurotics are discussed. Many of these issues have not been experimentally investigated and are presented in the light of subjective clinical impressions and experiences. The main argument put forward is the importance of active participation of the patient in planning and conducting his own treatment-programme. It is stressed that the patient should be given a detailed description of the treatment as well as a readily intelligible account of its theoretical background. The active role of the patient was also discussed in the context of voluntary controntation with feared situations, the patient's decision to accept treatment, the assessment of his motivation, the involvement of the patient's family in treatment, the arrangement of response prevention programmes and the problems of after care. Suggestions for further experimental investigation of some of the issues discussed are made.

REFERENCES

Boulougouris, J.C., and Bassiakos, L. (1973). Prolonged flooding in obsessive compulsive neuroses. Behaviour Research and Therapy, 10, 227-231.

Marks, I.M. (1975). Nurse therapists in behavioural psychotherapy. British Medical Journal, iii, 144-148.

Meyer-Gross W., Slater, E. and Roth M. (1969). Clinical Psychiatry, (3rd Ed.) Bailliere, Tindall and Cassel, London.

Meyer, V. and Chesser, E.S., (1970). Behaviour Therapy in Clinical Psychiatry, Harmondsworth, Penguin.

Rachman, S. Hodgson, R. and Marzillier, J. (1970). Treatment of obsessive compulsive disorder by modelling. Behaviour Research and Therapy, 8, 385-392.

Rachman, S., Hodgson, R. and Marks, I.M. (1971). The treatment of obsessive compulsive neurotics my modelling and flooding in-vivo. Behaviour Research and Therapy, 11, 463-471.

Roper, G., Rachman, S., and Marks, I.M. (1975). Passive and participant modelling in exposure treatment of obsessive compulsive neurotics. <u>Behaviour Research and Therapy</u>, 13, 271-279.

9. VARIABLES AFFECTING THE BEHAVIOUR MODIFICATION OF OBSESSIVE-COMPULSIVE PATIENTS TREATED BY FLOODING

John Boulougouris

Eginition Hospital, Department of Psychiatry, Athens University

Although flooding and modelling have proved to be effective therapy techniques on obsessive-compulsive states, clinical predictive measures of the outcome are insignificant (Marks, Hodgson and Rachman 1975).

On phobic disorders, which have been thoroughly studied during the past ten years, the prognostic variables to outcome with flooding are contradictory (Marks, Boulougouris and Marset 1971, Gelder, Bancroft, Gath, Johnston, Mathews and Shaw 1973). The need to obtain predictors to treatment response is most important, as the cost of therapy is high and there is a shortage of therapists. Patients' expectancy and variables, such as the modus operandi of the therapist, the encouragement provided and/or the challenges given to the patient during the treatment in-vivo, the duration and quality of exposure and particularly the home practice by the patients, are probably extremely important for the outcome. On the other hand, the systematic study of such variables is very difficult in patients under experimental trials and therefore the illustration of case studies, with such techniques, could throw more light, on the role of these variables to the outcome, than controlled experimental studies. In this paper an attempt is made to demonstrate some variables which are objective and measurable and which might prove useful to the treatment response with flooding in obsessive-compulsive patients. In addition, subjective ratings on the severity of symptoms and reports on the duration and form of symptoms, the presence or absence of mood swings and finally the constancy or the fluctuating course of the illness are also taken into consideration. Since some authors (Kringlen 1965, Pollit 1969) related the prognosis to the premorbid obsessional personality, the retrospective clinical assessment of the premorbid personality, as described by the patients, and its relationship to the outcome are also investigated in this paper. Nevertheless such measures as predictors to treatment response are really valid only when follow-up data show that the improvement is maintained after the end of treatment. Over the past five years we have treated over 25 obsessive-compulsive patients with flooding therapy and, in some, flooding was administered in combination with modelling and tricyclics. This paper presents data on 15 patients which have been followed-up systematically over the years and treated only with flooding. Correlations with some improvement criteria will be shown.

FOLLOW-UP DATA

The sample consisted of ten men and five women whose mean age was 29.4 years (SD=9.5) and their mean duration of symptoms was 8.7 years (SD=6.9). Twelve patients were treated under controlled experimental conditions to assess the optimum duration of flooding sessions in fantasy or "in-vivo" (Rabavilas, Boulougouris, Stefanis 1976, Boulougouris, Rabavilas and Stefanis 1977) and the remaining three were treated with prolonged flooding sessions in fantasy

and "in-vivo" (Boulougouris and Bassiakos 1973). These studies showed that
long flooding sessions in-vivo i.e. exposure for more than 90 minutes, were
superior to long or short fantasy sessions and to short practice sessions on
various clinical and physiological variables. A facilitating effect was found
of long fantasy sessions prior to exposure. It was also demonstrated that
treatment could be administered on an outpatient basis and that flooding in-
vivo could be started immediately.

The patients treated had a total of 11 sessions, most of them exposure in-vivo
and the mean follow-up was 2.8 years (range 2-5 years). They received similar
clinical assessments before treatment started, at the end of treatment and
at follow-up. In clinical ratings Fig. 9.1 and on Leyton Obsessional Inventory Fig. 9.2 , further improvement was found after the end of the treatment.

MAIN   OBSESSION

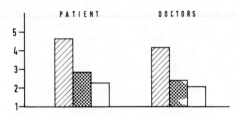

TOTAL   OBSESSIONS

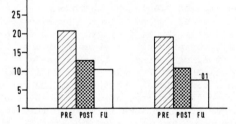

Fig. 9.1   Mean scores an patients and doctors ratings on main and
           total obsessions before treatment, after treatment and
           at follow-up.

The improvement at the follow-up on total obsessions as rated by the doctors
was significant compared to post treatment scores (P < .01).

On interference score, a similar improvement (P < .05) at the follow-up was
found when the follow-up scores were compared to post-treatment scores. The
scores before treatment, after treatment and at follow-up, according to the
patients' and doctors' ratings on anxiety and depression, were unchanged.

Of the 15 followed-up patients, 9 were found most improved and were almost
symptom free at the time of assessment. The rest were classified as least
improved. As a criterion taken for improvement was a reduction of more than
2 points on the main obsession according to the patients' ratings. The

patients found as most improved at the end of therapy (**Fig.** 9.3) showed significantly more improvement at the follow-up according to patients' ratings (P < .01) and on total obsessions according to doctors' ratings (P < .05).

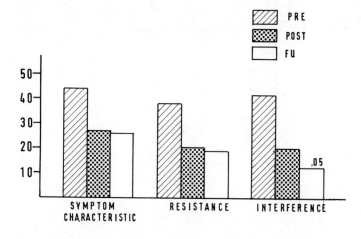

Fig. 9.2   Mean scores on Leyton Obsessional Inventory

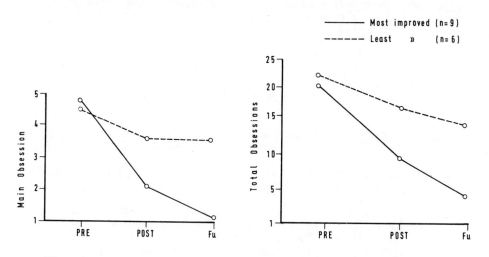

Fig.   9.3   Mean scores on main and total obsessions according
to patients for the most and least improved patients

The improved patients at the end of therapy, showed at follow-up a further
improvement (Fig. 9.4) on the Leyton interference score (P<.05) but not on
resistance score. The most improved patients had symptoms which consisted
mainly of cleaning rituals and had fears of contamination. In two out of
nine, ruminative thoughts were the main symptoms and in those patients the
occurrence of mood swings was reported. Furthermore, the course of their
illness was fluctuating. The seven improved patients did not exhibit mood
swings and their illness was constant without remissions and exacerbations.
All but two improved patients had anankastic premorbid personalities.

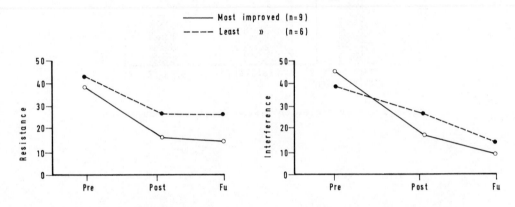

Fig. 9.4 Mean scores on resistance and interference scores of
           Leyton Obsessional Inventory for the most and least
           improved patients

In contrast, the form of the symptoms in the six unimproved patients consisted
mainly of ruminative thoughts (4) and checking behaviour (2). Mood swings
were present in four patients and in five the course of the illness was
fluctuating. Three out of six had an anankastic type, two histrionic and
one schizoid type of premorbid personality.

On ten patients, psychophysiological measures were taken before treatment, at
the end of treatment and at follow-up by the precedure described elsewhere
(Boulougouris, et al 1977). The reduction in autonomic reactivity, as measured by the changes in pulse rate, skin conductance maximum deflection and
spontaneous fluctuations during neutral and anxiety provoking situations,

are shown in Fig. 9.5. Even when significant reduction was found at the end
of treatment, no further reduction was recorded at the follow-up.   In subjective anxiety ratings (Fig. 9.6) during the psychophysiological procedure, a
significant reduction was found during the flooding "in-vivo" period (P < .001)
but much less was recorded during the obsessive fantasy period (P < .05).

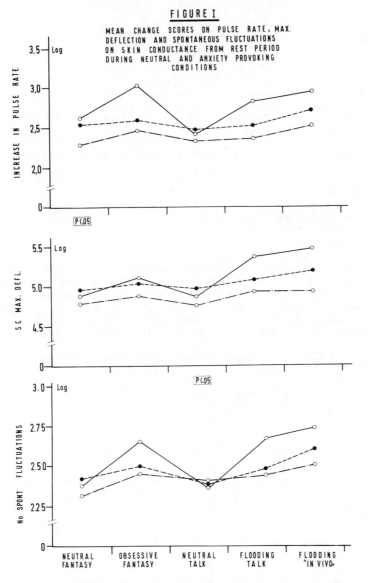

FIGURE I

MEAN CHANGE SCORES ON PULSE RATE, MAX.
DEFLECTION AND SPONTANEOUS FLUCTUATIONS
ON SKIN CONDUCTANCE FROM REST PERIOD
DURING NEUTRAL AND ANXIETY PROVOKING
CONDITIONS

Fig.   9.5   Mean change scores on pulse rate, maximum deflection
             and spontaneous fluctuations on skin conductance from
             rest period during neutral and anxiety provoking
             conditions

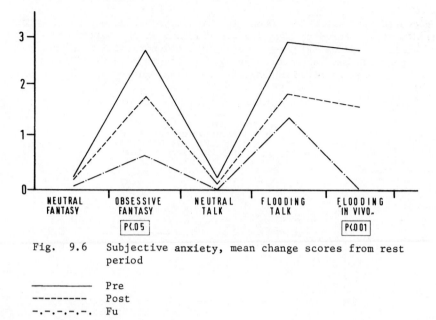

Fig. 9.6 Subjective anxiety, mean change scores from rest period

——————— Pre

- - - - - - - - Post

-.-.-.-.- Fu

PROGNOSTIC VARIABLES

On ten patients a correlation matrix was carried out with some improvement criteria (Table 9.1). The improvement criteria chosen were: main obsession (doctors' ratings), Leyton (interference score), skin conductance maximum deflection during obsessive fantasy, heart rate and number of spontaneous fluctuations during flooding talk period and heart rate as well as the number of spontaneous fluctuations during the flooding in-vivo period.

Table 9.1 Prognostic variables after flooding

CORRELATION WITH VARIABLES AT START OF TREATMENT	IMPROVEMENT CRITERIA												
	CLINICAL				PSYCHOPHYSIOLOGICAL								
	Main obsession (Doctors' Ratings) Post-trt.	FU	Leyton O.I. (interference) Post-trt.	FU	Obsessive fantasy S.C. max. defl Post-trt.	FU	Flooding talk Heart Rate Post-trt.	FU	S.C. Spont. fluct. Post-trt.	FU	Flooding "in vivo" Heart Rate Post-trt.	FU	S.C. Spont. fluct Post-trt.	FU
CLINICAL RATINGS MAIN OBSESSION (RATIENT)							.66*							
ANXIETY »					.64*	.72*							.85***	
DEPRESSION »				-.79**									.77**	
LEYTON OBSESSIONAL INV. SYMPTOM		-.84**		.76**										
INTERFERENCE		-.79**	.73*	.94***										
HEAR RATE OBSESSIVE FANTASY							.81**							
FLOODING "IN VIVO.													.67*	
S.C. SPONT. FLUCTUATIONS NEUTRAL FANTASY			.76**								.70*			
OBSESSIVE »									.74*					
NEUTRAL TALK									.71**					
FLOODING »									.78**		.60*		.83***	
» "IN VIVO"														
S.C. MAX. DEFLECTION NEUTRAL FANTASY			.67*											
OBSESSIVE »						.88*			.65*				.73*	
NEUTRAL TALK									.73*					
FLOODING "IN VIVO"														

Almost all correlations at the end of the treatment were positive and patients with the greater physiological arousal, during the neutral or high affect stimulation periods, showed the greatest improvement. Nevertheless, the correlations before treatment started with the same improvement criteria at follow-up were insignificant. Only the amount of free-floating anxiety rated by the patients was positively correlated with the improved skin conductance, maximum deflection during the obsessive fantasy period at the end of treatment (r=.64) and at the follow-up (r=.72). The absence of significant correlations at the follow-up compared to those at the end of therapy was disappointing. The prognosis was not correlated with sex, age, duration of illness and subjective anxiety experienced during the flooding therapy sessions.

In order to find other predictors to treatment response, a study on the anticipatory fear responses was carried out. The rationale of this study was based on the long standing clinical view that uncertainty occupied a central part in the obsessional symptomatology (Beech and Liddell 1974), and the suggestion that obsessive ruminations could be due to patients' inability to anticipate what will take place in various situations (Mather 1970). Concerning the theory of response uncertainty and arousal, much evidence exists that uncertain conditions elicit higher autonomic arousal than conditions of certainty (Berlyne 1960, Bowers 1971). Therefore the psychophysiological responses to the anticipation of physical danger and to individually determined psychological stress were investigated. In was surmised that obsessive-compulsive patients will have greater anticipatory fear responses than normal and probably patients with the greater responses before treatment will respond better to flooding therapy.

Eight chronic obsessive-compulsive patients before undergoing flooding therapy and eight controls, matched for age and sex, were studied. Each group consisted of three females and five males. Patients with obsessive and/or compulsive symptoms secondary to other illnesses (depressive, schizophrenic or organic) were excluded. The mean age was 29.5 years (range 21 to 45) and the mean duration of illness 7.6 years (range 1 to 15). Five patients were mainly compulsive washers and the other three were ruminators. The controls were physically and mentally healthy individuals. They were taken from the Hospital personnel and their mean age was 29 years (range 22 to 44).

As physical danger, a series of electric shocks was administered. The psychological threat was deduced from their psychiatric assessment. During the interview the single symptom which was the most disturbing was determined and the experimental "stress" involved confrontation of the patient with that situation, i.e. touching a "contaminating" object by a compulsive washer. In an obsessive ruminative case, the patient would listen to one of his distressing unacceptable thoughts. With regard to the psychological stress for the controls, they were asked during the interview to report their most significant experience, the occurence of which would make them emotionally upset. Such experiences were mainly the loss of their jobs due to incompetence, a sexual insult or a family disaster.

The study was conducted under 50% uncertainty manipulation and the stress situations were presented at random during three out of six trials. Pulse rate and skin conductance were measured while the detailed experimental procedure, as well as the scoring system have been described elsewhere (Rabavilas Boulougouris, Stefanis and Vaidakis 1976). Baseline measures and the scores, during the anticipation trials, were counted. Analysis of these data showed no significant differences on both baseline measures between the two groups. In shock anticipation, the heart rate changes were greater (P < .05) in patients than controls.

On psychological threat, the changes in heart rate did not discriminate between the groups. Skin conductance responses were greater in patients than controls in psychological threat and shock anticipation (both P < .01).

A series of t-tests between first and sixth trial on each group showed no significant decrements of heart rate on both groups for either nature of anticipation. The decrement of skin conductance between trials, was significantly greater (P < .001) in controls than patients.

The scores on fear anticipatory responses, before flooding started, were correlated with some improvement criteria at the end of therapy (Table 9.2).

Table 9.2   Correlations of anticipatory fear responses to shock and psychological threat before treatment with some improvement criteria after flooding

*   P < .05
**   P < .01
***   P < .001

ANTICIPATORY FEAR RESPONSES AT START		I m p r o v e m e n t		C r i t e r i a					
		CLINICAL		PSYCHOPHYSIOLOGICAL					
		Main obsession (Pts' Ratings)	Leyton O.I. (interference)	obsessive fantasy		flooding talk		flooding in v.v.o.	
				Heart Rate	S.C. max. defl.	Heart Rate	S.C. spont. fluct	Heart Rate	S.C. max. defl.
Shock	HEART RATE	−.21	−.25	.01	.45	.81*	.59	.17	.66
	S.C. MAX. DEFL.	.01	.3	.04	.86**	.67	.57	.10	.73*
Psychological Threat	HEART RATE	−.14	−.51	10	.55	.58	.52	.14	.63
	S.C. MAX. DEFL.	.10	−.64	.21	.98***	.43	.37	.45	.72*

The correlation matrix revealed no significant correlations of anticipatory fear responses with the clinical criteria of improvement. Related to the physiological improvement criteria, it was found that patients with the greater responses on shock anticipation, improved most in skin conductance responses during the obsessive fantasy testing period (r= .86, P < .05) and during the flooding in-vivo testing period (r= .73, P < .05). Similar positive correlations were found between the responses on psychological threat anticipation and improvement on skin conductance during the obsessive fantasy testing period (r= .98, P < .001) and during flooding in-vivo period (r= .72, P < .05). Heart rate at the beginning of shock anticipation studies was correlated with the heart rate responses during the flooding talk testing period (r= .81, P < .01). It remains to be seen if similar correlations can be found at the follow-up testing.

DISCUSSION

The data confirm the findings from other studies (Meyer, Levy and Schnurer

1974, Hackman and Mclean 1975, Roper, Rachman and Marks 1975, Marks et al 1975)
that the improvement obtained, from the administration of behavioural methods
in obsessive-compulsive patients, is maintained. The validity of these data
could be argued since no control group was used and the clinical assessment
was not blind. On the other hand, it could not be denied that obsessive-compulsive disorder was one of the most resistant to any treatment intervention.
The dramatic breakthrough in 1970 (Rachman, Hodgson and Marzillier 1970) by
the application of behavioural methods has been greeted with great enthusiasm.
In all these methods (apotreptic, flooding, modelling) the common factor is
exposure in-vivo with response prevention. Prolonged exposure to the threatening situations is advisable. Patients need firm persuasion from their therapist, whose style seems to play a great part in the treatment to enter into
threatening situations (Hodgson 1976). The therapist would be wise to be
cautious in describing the next step of exposure in-vivo in order not to raise
excessively the anticipation anxiety which is common in these patients, as
was shown in this study, and may prevent their attending the session. Such
precautions help to provide the patients with enthusiasm to face threatening
situations and to feel that they have successfully tolerated their anxiety
without performing their rituals.

Patients who had improved at the end of therapy showed further improvement
at the follow-up. The improvement was attributed by the patients to the
treatment itself, since they had learned to cope with a stressful situation
and consequently they reported practicing according to the instructions
given during the treatment. All patients were instructed to continue rehear-
sing the manifestation beyond any point of necessity suggested by their illness whenever they had succumbed to the demands of an obsessive compulsion.
All improved patients reported that the continuous practice after the end of
their therapy diminished their fear of contamination or loss of control and
therefore it was not necessary to perform their rituals.

The physiological investigation showed a greater reduction of autonomic
reactivity during the flooding in-vivo testing periods than during the fantasy periods. Such findings support the experimental data of Simpson and Pavio
(1966) that quicker extinction occurs in the external or concrete stimuli
than in the internal or abstract stimuli. Although the patients were found
on clinical ratings considerably improved at the follow-up, the physiological
improvement was not so marked. In addition the minimal decrease of arousal
during the obsessive imagery could be due to cognitive mediational processes
(Katkin and Murray 1966). Such processes probably inhibit or facilitate the
physiological responses to various incoming stimuli and therefore further
investigation on these lines could provide some support for a neuronal model
(Sokolov 1963) of explaining this disability.

The greater autonomic responses found during anticipation of threatening stimuli is of some interest. Although such findings do not support the notion
that obsessive-compulsive patients function at rest with an abnormal state of
arousal (Beech and Liddel 1974), they indicate that autonomic reactivity differs in these patients from controls. Opposite to what is usually found in
psychopaths (Hare 1970) it was clear that in obsessive-compulsive patients
cues associated with future punishment are generating greater fear anticipatory responses than controls. However, similar responses can be found in
anxiety states and it seems unlikely that such patterns of autonomic responses
are specific to obsessive-compulsive patients. The autonomic reactivity is

probably fluctuating and determined by environmental factors as well. This view is supported by the author's experience derived from some patients who before having had psychotherapy had almost autonomic silence to various threatening situations. After psychotherapy they exhibited intense autonomic responses to the same situations. The resistance for significant decrement over trials of both measures is probably most important and provides more grounds for a further study on the rate of habituation on those patients and their response to treatment.

Regarding the prognostic factors tested in this study it can be said that only the form of symptoms is the best indicator of treatment response:i.e. patients with washing rituals respond to flooding therapy better than patients with obsessions and checking behaviour. Similar response to treatment has been shown by others (Marks et al 1975) and therefore the development of new methods of treatment for obsessional ruminations is needed (Rachman 1976). Furthermore, the steady course of the illness, the absence of mood swings and the obsessional type of premorbid personality might be related to good outcome. However, a systematic investigation of these variables is needed before using them as predictors to treatment response. The present study did not replicate at the follow-up previous findings that the more physiologically anxious patients did best with flooding (Boulougouris et al 1977). The positive correlations found with the anticipatory fear responses need to be found at the follow-up as well before using them as predictors to treatment response. From a psychopathological point of view the knowledge about the effects on many systems of expectancy violations, threatening stimuli and conditions of certainty or uncertainty are worth searching for in order to understand this puzzling nosological entity.

SUMMARY

Fifteen patients with chronic obsessive-compulsive rituals were treated with flooding in fantasy and "in-vivo". The mean number of treatment sessions was eleven. Nine out of the fifteen were much improved, almost symptom free and they maintained their improvement after 2.8 years follow-up. Patients with cleaning rituals, absence of mood swings and continuous course of their illness responded to treatment. Patients with ruminations, checking behaviour, mood swings and periods of remissions did not respond. Physiological measures as predictors to the flooding outcome should be seen with caution and it is early to say that patients with high autonomic reactivity to threatening or neutral stimuli respond best to flooding therapy.

ACKNOWLEDGEMENTS

I am grateful to Dr. A.D. Rabavilas and N. Vaidakis who treated some patients and helped me in the analysis of the data.

REFERENCES

Beech, H.R. and Liddell, A. (1974). Decision-making, mood states and ritualistic behaviour among obsessional patients. In H. R. Beech (Ed.) Obsessional States, 143-160, Methuen.

Berlyne, D.E. (1960). Conflict, Arousal and Curiosity, McGraw Hill, New York.

Boulougouris, J.C. and Bassiakos L. (1973). Prolonged flooding in obsessive compulsive neurosis. Behaviour Research and Therapy, 10, 227-231.

Boulougouris, J.C., Rabavilas, A.D., and Stefanis C., (1977). Psychophysiological responses in obsessive-compulsive patients. Behaviour Research and Therapy, (in press).

Bowers, K.S., (1971). Heart rate and GSR, concomitants of vigilance and arousal. Canadian Journal of Psychiatry, 25, 175-185.

Gelder, M.G., Bancroft J.H.J., Gath D.H., Johnston D.W., Mathews A.M., and Shaw P.M., (1973). Specific and non-specific factors in behavior therapy. British Journal of Psychiatry, 123, 445-462.

Hackman, A., and McLean, C., (1975). A comparison of flooding and thought stopping in the treatment of obsessional neurosis. Behaviour Research and Therapy, 13, 263-269.

Hare, R.D., (1965). Temporal gradient of fear arousal in psychopaths. Journal of Abnormal Psychology, 10, 6, 442-445.

Hodgson, R., (1976). Personal communication.

Katkin, E.S., and Murray, E.N., (1968). Instrumentation of autonomically mediated behaviour: Theoretical and methodological issues. Psychological Bulletin, 70, 52-68.

Kringle, N.E., (1965). Obsessional neurotics. A long-term follow-up. British Journal of Psychiatry, 2, 709-22.

Marks, I.M., Boulougouris J.C., and Marset, P., (1971). Flooding versus desensitisation in phobic disorders. British Journal of Psychiatry, 119, 353-375.

Marks, I.M. Hodgson, R, and Rachman, S., (1975). Treatment of chronic obsessive-compulsive neurosis by in-vivo exposure, British Journal of Psychiatry, 127, 349-64.

Mather, D.M., (1970). The treatment of an obsessive-compulsive patient by discrination learning and reinforcement of decision-making. Behaviour Research and Therapy, 8, 315-318.

Meyer, V., Levy, R., and Schnuner, A., (1974). The behavioural treatment of obsessive-compulsive disorders. In H.R. Beech (Ed.) Obsessional States, 233-258, Methuen.

Pollit, J. (1969). Obsessional states. British Journal of Hospital Medicine, 2, 1146-50.

Rabavilas, A.D., Boulougouris, J.C., and Stefanis C. (1976). Duration of flooding sessions in the treatment of obsessive-compulsive patients. Behaviour Research and Therapy, 14, 349-355.

Rabavilas, A.D., Boulougouris, J.C., Vaidakis, N., and Stefanis C., (1977).

Psychophysiological accompaniments of threat anticipation in obsessive compulsive patients.   In C.D. Spielberger and I.G. Sarason (Eds.) Stress and
Anxiety, Vo. 4.   Hemisphere Publications Corporation, Washington D.C.

Rachman, S., Hodgson, R. and Marzillier, J., (1970).   Treatment of an obsessional disorder by modelling.   Behaviour Research and Therapy, 8, 385-92.

Rachman, S. (1976).   The modification of obsessions: A new formulation.   Behaviour Research and Therapy, 14, 437-443.

Roper, G., Rachman S. and Marks, I.M., (1975).   Passive and participant modelling in exposure treatment of obsessive-compulsive neurotics.   Behaviour
Research and Therapy, 13, 271-279.

Simpson, A.M., and Pavio, A. (1966).   Changes in pupil size during an imagery
task without motor response involvement.   Psychonomic Science, 5, 405-406.

Sokolov, Y.N., (1963).   Perception and the Conditioned Reflex, Oxford, Pergamon Press.

10. THE EFFECTIVENESS OF FOUR BEHAVIOUR THERAPIES IN THE TREATMENT OF OBSESSIVE NEUROSIS

Debbie Sookman and Leslie Solyom

Allan Memorial Institute, Montreal, Canada

INTRODUCTION

Obsessive neurosis is a complex, debilitating disorder which, up until recently, has been very resistant to treatment. In the absence of any one acceptable encompassing theory to explain the disorder, attempts to treat it have varied greatly in conceptualization and technique. The behavioural treatment for obsessive neurosis has involved a host of treatments, including such disparate measures as systematic desensitisation and flooding with response prevention, paradoxical intention, social reinforcement and punishment, covert sensitization, as well as modelling, aversion relief, and thought stopping. Meyer, Levy and Schnurer (1974) reviewed the results of behavioural techniques up until 1971 and found them unimpressive with only a 55% improvement rate. Recently, behavioural techniques have been developed which seem to produce better results, particularly in patients with rituals, with the use of prolonged exposure and response prevention administered to in-patients (Meyer et al 1974; Marks, Hodgson and Rachman, 1975).

The applicability of these techniques to all obsessives may be questionable, however, as the treated patients all had compulsions and those whose major symptomatology was ruminations were excluded. However, obsessive neurosis is phenomenologically a heterogenous disorder: the predominance of ruminations, rituals, horrific temptations, and doubt differs from patient to patient. Symptoms belonging to other nosological categories are also not infrequently present in obsessive neurosis. As Pujol and Savy (1968) remark: "Elle est situee au carrefour dela melancholie et della paranoia d'un cote, des diverses formes d' hysterie de l'autre, sans oublier dans une troisieme direction les perversions et les caracteres psychopathiques." Akhtar and his associates (1975) have differentiated those patients whose primary symptoms are obsessive phobias and horrific temptations from those who suffer mostly from fear of contamination and rituals. Straus (1948) suggested that patients with horrific temptations tend towards a more benign course. There is evidence that even the type of ritual may determine outcome: "checking" being more resistant to treatment with flooding or modelling than "hand washing" (Rachman, Hodgson and Marks, 1971).

The need for empirical data on the differential effectiveness of behavioural techniques in ameliorating each type of obsessive symptom motivated this study. Our purpose was to assess the relative effectiveness of four behaviour therapy techniques: aversion relief, flooding, thought stopping, and a combination of systematic desensitization and thought stopping on each of the four cardinal symptoms of obsessive neurosis: ruminations, rituals, horrific temptations, and pervading doubt. Having learned more about the specificity of treatment on the above symptom clusters and on other neurotic features, it was our intention to develop a broad spectrum behaviour therapy suited to each individual patient.

85

METHOD

Subjects

All patients were referred from out-patient departments of the teaching hospitals of McGill University and University of Ottawa, who presented obsessive symptoms as their primary complaint. Those individuals presenting symptoms of clinical depression, schizophrenia, or organic brain damage in addition to the obsessive symptoms were not included in the study. All other obsessive patients, regardless of the duration of illness, initial severity of symptomatology, age, etc., were accepted for treatment. The total sample size was 33.

Assessment measures

1.   Each patient was given a full psychiatric assessment with the use of a standardized questionnaire. The four main obsessive symptom clusters were rated on a 0-4 point scale and a quantitative measure of the frequency (e.g. number of daily hand washings) and severity (ranging from mild to incapacitating) were obtained for each obsessive symptom. Other psychiatric syndromes, such as depression, general anxiety, hysteria, hypochondriasis, etc., were rated on a 1-5 point scale. Each score here represents the composite average of 4-7 symptoms characteristic of the syndrome. Other descriptive and phenomenological data, such as the patient's family background, premorbid personality, history of present and past illnesses and treatment, etc. were also obtained.

2.   Each patient filled out two self-assessment forms, which rated:(a) each obsessive symptom, the main phobia, and other neurotic symptoms and (b) social adjustment to work, leisure, extra and intra-familial relationships, and sexual adjustment on a 1-5 point scale. Severity of symptoms and degree of social maladjustment were also operationally defined for each point.

3.   The psychometric tests used uncluded the IPAT Manifest Anxiety Scale, the Fear Survey Schedule (Wolpe and Lang, 1964), the Maudsley Personality Inventory, and the Leyton Obsessional Inventory (Cooper, 1970). The Leyton Obsessional Inventory is probably the best measure of obsessive symptoms to date and yields an obsessive symptom score and an obsessive trait score, as well as a measure of the resistance to and interference from the obsessive symptoms*

After initial assessment, the patients were matched on four criteria: age, sex education, and duration of illness and were assigned pseudo-randomly to one of the four treatment groups. There were 8 patients in the aversion relief, thought stopping, and systematic desensitization andthought stopping groups and 9 patients in the flooding group. An attempt was made to assign the

---

*   The Leyton, as an assessment tool, has two weaknesses:(1) it does not equally represent the four symptom clusters, as only three questions on this scale relate to horrific temptations. A recent factor analytic study we carried out indicated that over 40% if the variance on the pre-treatment resistance and interference components was accounted for by questions pertaining to rituals. (2) It does not accurately reflect the degree of incapacity suffered by a patient with only a few severe obsessive symptoms (as in the case of one patient whose single ritual lasted all day and in itself incapacitated him.)

patients such that obsessive symptomatology was similar from group to group.
Although in a clinical study of this kind, intergroup homogeneity could be
only partially achieved, we nevertheless managed to assign patients with
very similar symptoms to different groups. For example, in both the flooding
and the thought stopping groups there was a patient whose main ruminations
centered around the shape of his/her nose; in both the aversion relief and
thought stopping groups there was one patient whose most incapacitating
symptom consisted of a long-lasting, ritualistic cleaning of the house
every night. Four illustrative case histories are presented in the Appendix.

Each patient received 50 treatment sessions, 50 minutes duration each, twice
weekly and was assessed prior to and on completion of treatment. No patient
was on medication while receiving behaviour therapy.

Treatment techniques

Aversion relief group:

In the aversion relief (AR) group, five different tape-recorded narratives
and/or slides or films of each patient's obsessive experiences were used
in the treatment program. During their presentation, anxiety-provoking stimuli and anxiety responses were coupled with aversion relief produced by
patient-controlled cessation of finger electric shock. In the treatment of
six patients, we used only the tape recorded texts. In two more cases texts
as well as films of the obsessive rituals were used. In these latter cases,
aversion relief was also administered in vivo (e.g. finger electric shock
stopped when the patient touched the "contaminated" object).

Flooding group:

The five narratives prepared by each patient in the flooding (FL) group provided cues to describe a "terrifying", highly exaggerated account of an obsessive
experience which was tape-recorded by the therapist and presented to the
patient for an uninterrupted session of 45–50 minutes. New flooding themes
were introduced when the originals failed to produce anxiety in the patient.
In two cases, treatment was restricted to flooding in imagination (e.g. the
patient imagined enacting an anxiety-provoking horrific temptation). In the
remaining six cases, treatment consisted of a combination of flooding in
imagination, an audio-visual description of the obsessive experience, and in
vivo flooding. Since the nature of the symptoms dictated the mode of in vivo
flooding, the treatment for this group of patients was less homogenous than
for the other three groups. Patients were encouraged to refrain from carrying
out their compulsions and to resist their ruminations, etc. Feedback and
social praise were provided, but stringent supervision was not attempted.
This would have been impractical as, unlike other studies previously reported,
only a minority of the patients were hospitalized. Emphasis was thus placed
more on exposure than on response prevention.

Thought stopping group:

Ruminations leading to a ritual or creating great anxiety due to their aggressive content were listed in distinct phrases for the thought stopping (TS)
group. The patient was asked to think over these obsessive thoughts twice,
signalling when he had done so by lifting his right index finger. At this
point the therapist administered finger shock and shouted "stop". Gradually

the electric shock was eliminated and the word "stop" was taken over by the patient himself. The treatment was a modified version of the thought stopping treatment described by Stern (1970). Where appropriate, aversion was also applied in a successive manner to the image of the stimuli which provoked the obsessive ruminations and to the imagery of the obsessive ritual as well.

Systematic desensitisation and thought stopping group:

In the systematic desensitisation and thought stopping (SD + TS) group, patients first received 15 therapy sessions to desensitize them to the cues which provoked their obsessive behaviour. This treatment sequence was designed with the hypothesis that it would be easier to eliminate the obsessive rumination on ritual if the stimulus which provoked the symptom in the sequence stimulus-rumination-ritual was weakened by the desensitisation therapy.

RESULTS

The means of the matching criteria are shown in Table 10.1. The mean duration of illness was 13 years.

Table 10.1   Means on matching criteria

	A R		F L		T S		SD + TS		TOTAL POPULATION	
	Mean	Range	Mean	Range	Mean	Range	Mean	Range	Mean	Range
Number of Patients	8		9		8		8		33	
Sex M:F	4:4		4:5		6:2		5:3		19:14	
Age	38.1	(21-54)	36.4	(20-59)	32.0	(21-43)	31.4	(17-46)	34.5	(17-59)
Education (years)	11.5	(9-14)	11.9	(9-15)	14.5	(11-19)	11.6	(6-18)	12.4	(6-19)
Duration of Illness (years)	11.0	(1-28)	15.9	(4-35)	13.6	(2-34)	11.4	(3-39)	13.1	(1-39)

Reference to Table 10.2 shows that the mean age of onset of the disorder (when the present symptomatology became stable) was 22.

Table 10.2   Course of obsessive neurosis and impairment of function at time of study

	A R	F L	T S	SD + TS	TOTAL POPULATION
	n = 8	n = 9	n = 8	n = 8	N = 33
Mean age of onset of illness	27.1	20.7	18.4	20.4	21.6
Course:					
No. of patients with:					
Constant static	0	0	0	2 (25.0%)	2 (6.1%)
Constant worsening	4 (50.0%)	4 (44.4%)	3 (37.5%)	2 (25.0%)	13 (39.4%)
Fluctuating	2 (25.0%)	4 (44.4%)	4 (50.0%)	4 (50.0%)	14 (42.4%)
Phasic	2 (25.0%)	1 (11.1%)	1 (12.5%)	0	4 (12.1%)
Impairment of function:					
No. of patients:					
Unimpaired	3 (37.5%)	0	0	0	3 (9.1%)
Somewhat disabled	3 (37.5%)	3 (33.3%)	7 (87.5%)	7 (87.5%)	20 (60.6%)
Incapacitated	3 (37.5%)	6 (66.7%)	1 (12.5%)	1 (12.5%)	11 (33.3%)

Thereafter, only 4 of the 33 patients reported experiencing a symptom-free
period. The majority had suffered from unremitting symptomatology for over
a decade, 13 showing progressive worsening. Eleven patients (33%) were
totally disabled by their obsessive neurosis and could no longer function
at their jobs. Ten had to be hospitalized despite the critical shortage
of beds. Table 10.3 shows the incidence of occurence of obsessive symptoms.

Table 10.3   Incidence of obsessive symptoms

Number of patients with	A R n = 8	F L n = 9	T S n = 8	SD + TS n = 8	TOTAL POPULATION N = 33
Ruminations	6 (75.0%)	9 (100%)	7 (87.5%)	7 (87.5%)	29 (87.9%)
Rituals	8 (100%)	7 (77.8%)	6 (75.0%)	6 (75.0%)	21 (63.6%)
Horrific temptations	6 (75.0%)	6 (66.7%)	5 (62.5%)	3 (37.5%)	20 (60.6%)
Pervading doubt	5 (62.5%)	7 (77.8%)	8 (100%)	7 (87.5%)	27 (81.8%)
All obsessive symptoms	4 (50.0%)	5 (55.6%)	3 (37.5%)	2 (25.0%)	14 (42.4%)

With exception of 2, all patients who had ruminations had rituals as well.
Overall, ruminations and doubt were the most commonly occurring symptoms.
As no pre-selection was made on the basis of symptomatology, 42% of the patients presented all the cardinal symptoms of obsessive neurosis - ruminations, rituals, horrific temptations, and doubt. On the average, the patients
had three previous treatments before consulting us for an average total period
of three years. Of those patients who had received prior psychotherapy (78%),
60% claimed to have derived no benefit. Only one half of the patients, who
had been treated pharmacologically (neuroleptic or anti-depressant medication
mostly), felt that they had benefited from this. Of the seven patients who
had received ECT, five showed temporary benefit.

There were no significant inter-group differences in the incidence or initial
severity of obsessive symptoms on any of the assessment measures. Overall,
behaviour therapy significantly reduced the obsessive symptomatology in this
chronically ill sample by 33% (p<.01). Pervading doubt was significantly
reduced by 53% (p < .001). There was also a reduction of 22–32% in ruminations,
rituals, and horrific temptations. To elucidate the results, the pre-post
treatment differences were translated into mean percentage of improvement.
Fig. 10.1 shows the mean pre and post treatment scores in the severity of
the obsessive-compulsive symptoms for the four treatment groups. The greatest
improvement in total obsessive symptomatology occurred in the flooding and
thought stopping groups, where there was a reduction of 50% in the total
obsessive symptoms. The application of systematic desensitisation and thought
stopping resulted in a 22% drop in obsessive symptomatology. Aversion relief
was ineffective, reducing the severity of the obsessive symptoms by a
clinically insignificant 5%.

The symptom clusters tended to show a differential response to treatment.

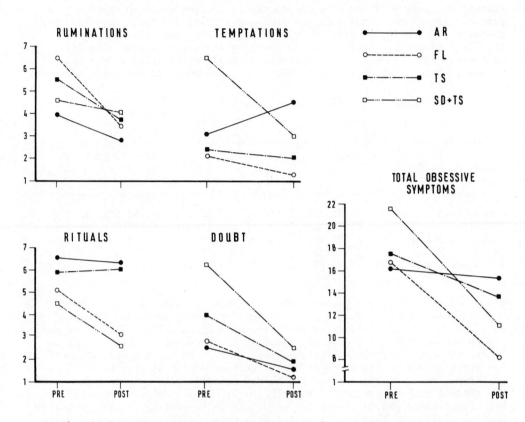

Fig. 10.1   Mean pre post treatment scores in severity of obsessive
symptoms.   Psychiatrist's rating

Ruminations and horrific temptations improved most when treated with flooding,
while rituals were most effectively reduced by thought stopping (46%, 84%, and
64%, resp.).   However, there was no sifnificant relationship in degree of
improvement among the symptom clusters.   That is, improvement in one treated
symptom or cluster of symptoms, e.g., rituals, was not significantly associated with a reduction in other untreated obsessive symptoms, e.g., ruminations.
Improvement did not generalise significantly to other clinical features, such
as phobias, unless the latter was treated directly.   There was no significant
correlation between initial severity of the obsessive symptoms and outcome.

On the Leyton Obsessive Inventory the overall behaviour therapy effect on the
total population was a decrease in the symptom score of a mean 24%   (p < .001)
and in interference score of a mean of 36%   (p < .0001).   In other words,
while the number of symptoms were only moderately reduced by treatment, their

duration or intensity was reduced so that they interfered considerably less
with the patient's life than previously.   A drop of 22% (p < .05) in the
resistance score occurred with the drop in number of symptoms as would be
expected.   There was no significant change in the obsessive trait score.
The effects of the different treatments on Leyton Obsessive Inventory are
illustrated in Fig. 10.2 and the evident reduction in interference score is
in the thought stopping group, where there was the greatest reduction in
rituals.

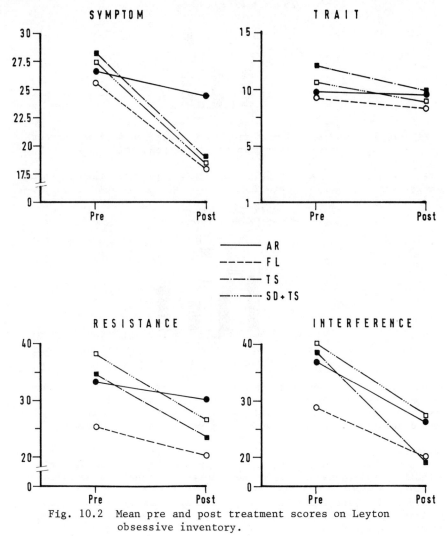

Fig. 10.2   Mean pre and post treatment scores on Leyton
            obsessive inventory.

There was a significant reduction in the patients' overall anxiety level,
(p < .001) as measured by the IPAT manifest anxiety scale, fearfulness (p < .05)
as measured by the FSS, degree of neuroticism, (p < .01), and a corresponding
increase in degree of extroversion as a result of behaviour therapy.   Consis-

tent with the other results, the flooding and thought stopping groups showed
the greatest reduction in anxiety level and in overall fearfulness.

On patients' self-ratings of their neurotic symptoms Fig. 10.3 significant
improvement was found in their main obsessive fear, often the focus of therapy
(33%), in their overall obsessive symptomatology (28%) and other neurotic
symptoms.

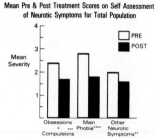

Fig. 10.3   Mean pre and post treatment scores on self assessment
of neurotic symptoms for total population

Patients in the flooding and thought stopping groups rated themselves as
being more improved than patients in the other groups as well, Fig. 10.4.

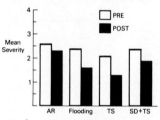

Fig. 10.4   Mean pre and post treatment scores on self assessment
of obsessive compulsive symptoms

The significant concordance rate (p < .01) in degree of improvement which
emerged on our three measures of obsessionality - the psychiatrist's ratings,
the Leyton Obsessive Inventory, and the patients' self-ratings is evidence
that our assessment measures constituted a valid index of outcome.

The patients rated themselves as significantly improved after all treatments
in their total social adjustment (33%, p < .001). With the exception of
intra-familial relationships, which were initially the least impaired by
the obsessive neurosis, all the other areas of social functioning significantly improved. Reducing the debilitating obsessive-compulsive symptoms allowed
the patient to resume a more normal life style. Table 10.4 shows that
patients in the flooding group rated themselves as most improved (by 54%).
Surprisingly, patients in the thought stopping group saw themselves as less
improved in their social functioning than patients in the systematic desensitisation and thought stopping group (20% and 50%) respectively).

Table 10.4   Mean pre and post treatment scores and percent
improvement in social maladjustment patients'
Patients' self rating

*   p < .05
**   p < .01
***   p< .001

	A R			F L			T S			SD + TS			TOTAL POPULATION		
	Pre	Post	%	Pre	Post	%	Pre	Post	%	Pre	Post	%	Pre	Post	%
Work or housework	1.9	1.8	6.9	3.1	1.5	52.1	1.6	1.3	23.3	2.9	1.7	40.2	1.9	1.8	6.9**
Leisure	2.4	1.3	47.5	1.9	0.9	53.2	2.0	1.1	43.5	2.0	1.3	35.5	2.1	1.1	45.1***
Sexual	1.9	1.7	8.1	2.3	1.3	44.4	1.4	1.1	18.1	0.8	0.4	50.0	1.6	1.2	28.0**
Intrafamilial	1.5	2.0	-33.3	1.5	0.8	50.0	1.1	1.1	0.0	1.6	1.4	8.9	1.4	1.3	7.0
Extrafamilial	2.9	2.1	10.5	2.3	0.9	60.9	2.0	1.8	12.5	1.7	1.1	33.3	2.1	1.5	29.5*
Lack of self-expression	2.8	2.6	444	3.0	1.3	58.3	2.1	1.9	11.7	2.3	2.0	12.7	2.5	1.9	23.6**
TOTAL	2.2	2.0	9.6	2.3	1.1	53.6	1.7	1.4	19.5	1.7	0.8	50.0	2.0	1.4	32.6***

The psychiatrist's assessment of the patient's total response to treatment
is shown in Table 10.5.   No patient was totally symptom free at termination.

Table 10.5   Psychiatrist's rating of total response to treatment

	A R	F L	T S	SD + TS	TOTAL POPULATION
Number of patients	n = 8	n = 9	n = 8	n = 8	N = 33
Socially adapted but still experiencing mild symptoms	3 (37.5%)	4 (44.4%)	5 (62.5%)	2 (25.0%)	14 (42.4%)
Poorly adapted socially but symptoms improved	2 (25.0%)	3 (33.3%)	2 (25.0%)	4 (50.0%)	11 (33.3%)
Symptoms worse or as severe as when first seen	3 (37.5%)	2 (22.2%)	1 (12.5%)	2 (25.0%)	8 (24.2%)

Fourteen of the 33 patients (42%) were rated as "much improved", i.e. socially
adapted, but still experiencing mild symptoms.   Four of these were in the
flooding group and five were in the thought stopping group.   Eleven patients
were improved in terms of their obsessive symptomatology, but were poorly
socially adapted.   Of the eleven, who were initially incapacitated, all but
one were returned to adequate functioning.

Eight patients showed no response to treatment.   A separate analysis is
presently being carried out to determine how these patients differed sympto-

matically and phenomenologically. These seemed to be the patients who showed
an earlier age to onset, suffered from more bizzare obsessional fears, and
showed less resistance to them perhaps a function of their higher anxiety
level.

DISCUSSION

This study differs from previous treatment studies in that its primary aim
was to determine the differential effectiveness of four widely used behaviour
therapy techniques in ameliorating each of the obsessive-compulsive symptom
clusters. For this reason (a) no pre-selection of treatment was made on
the basis of the type of severity of the presenting obsessive symptomatology
(b) assignment of patients to each of the four treatment groups was carried
out as randomly as was feasible in a clinical study of this kind, and (c) the
majority of patients treated were severely disabled, highly anxious people,
who showed a history of chronic multiple obsessive symptomatology which had
shown little response to previous psychotherapeutic, pharmacological, or
other somatic intervention.

Flooding and thought stopping were more effective overall than aversion relief
and a combination of systematic desensitisation and thought stopping, but were
not equally effective in reducing each of the obsessive-compulsive symptom
clusters: flooding was most effective in reducing the severity of ruminations
and horrific temptations, while rituals were most effectively reduced by
thought stopping. The fact that thought stopping was applied not only to
the patients' ruminations but also to the stimuli which provoked the ruminations (and rituals) as well as to the imagery of the rituals may explain its
effectiveness on the latter symptom. The question of whether the active
ingredient in prolonged exposure lies in the exposure itself or in the
response prevention associated with it awaits further empirical investigation.
Certainly thought stopping contains elements of both. In this study, dis-
rupting the obsessive thought pattern significantly reduced the overt ritualistic behaviour. Thought stopping may also reduce an important source of
secondary anxiety in the patient when he learns he can control some of his
obsessive unintended thoughts or urges to perform his rituals. Although this
was not directly assessed, thought stopping may have been more effective than
flooding in helping the patient to reduce his avoidance behaviour and to
maintain self-imposed response prevention at home.

The nature and content of the obsessive fear seemed important in determining
the effectiveness of treatment. Obsessive experiences or fears which were
less stimulus bound and more a function of the patient's fluctuating anxiety
level (for example, a horrific temptation, "what if I harm my husband", an
obsessive body image distortion, or pervading doubt and indecision) tended
to respond best to flooding, while thought stopping was most effective in
treating stimulus-provoked obsessive fears. The fact that ruminations, and
in particular horrific temptations, showed so much improvement in the flooding
group is encouraging as this has been the symptom cluster which has met with
less success (and attention) in the literature.

It is a common finding that relaxation in itself is ineffective in reducing
obsessive symptoms (Furst and Cooper, 1970; Marks et al 1975). A combination
of systematic desensitisation and thought stopping seemed to be anti-thera-
peutic, as the sequential application of both techniques was less effective
than thought stopping alone. This may have been due to the operation of a

"cognitive set" evoked by the prior treatment, which could have rendered the patient less amenable to subsequent aversive therapy. In systematic desensitisation the patient was taught to respond with relaxation to the cues which provoked his compulsive behaviour, while in thought stopping his ruminative response to these cues was evoked, but was associated with aversion.

It is perhaps not surprising that the application of aversion relief to the patients' taped narratives was not sufficient to counter-condition the intense compelling obsessive symptoms of these patients. It should be noted, however, that aversion relief applied in-vivo (i.e., when the patient actually stopped his ritual) or to visual stimuli (e.g., to a film in which the patient was seen carrying out his rituals) was much more successful, especially when associated with self-imposed response prevention at home.

The fact that there was no significant relationship in degree of improvement among the obsessive symptom clusters even though nearly half the patients suffered from all four types of obsessive symptoms strongly suggests that if our treatment is to be optimally effective, it should be directed towards each of the presenting obsessive symptoms. The behaviour therapy techniques, as they were applied in this study, substantially reduced the malignant obsessive-compulsive symptomatology - the ruminations, rituals, horrific temptations, pervading doubt and the interfering quality of these symptoms. After treatment patients showed more resistance to the symptoms which still remained (they were more able to resist the urge to recheck or to "decontaminate" themselves in the face of anxiety or doubt), and their recovery rate improved so much that their response to an anxiety provoking incident which prior to treatment might have persisted a day or as long as a few weeks, lasted only an hour or sometimes only a few minutes after treatment. To date more than one half of the patients have been reassessed at six months and one year after treatment, and many have continued to improve. There have been no relapses. However, none of the patients were symptom-free after treatment. Improvement did not generalize to other neurotic symptoms, such as phobias, and was not associated with improved social functioning in all cases. Many patients maintained other, less severe neurotic symptoms after treatment and continued to manifest obsessive personality traits - notably a lack of adaptability, repetitiveness, and concern with cleanliness, order, and routine. About one third of the successfully treated patients required booster treatments at bi-weekly or monthly intervals, or when they were under strees in order to maintain their improvement.

These results underline the need for a broad spectrum approach to the treatment of obsessive neurosis. Obsessive-compulsive symptoms are often both self-reinforcing and anxiety augmenting, and often constantly worsening due to generalization to seemingly unrelated cues (Reed, 1968; Solyom et al, 1971; Beech, 1971). There is evidence that recurrence of symptoms between treatment sessions is detrimental (Walton and Mather, 1963). A broad spectrum approach would involve the joint application of several behavioural techniques considered to be most effective in alleviating each of the presenting obsessive symptom clusters in any given patient. The treatment paradigm applied in each case would be determined by the quality and content of each of the obsessive symptoms, in relation to other symptoms and to anxiety, etc. Reinforcement schedules, self-monitoring, involvement of the family etc. should be used to help the patient carry out self-imposed response prevention at home as an essential adjunct to treatment in the hospital or office.

There is some evidence that self-imposed response prevention at home can be as effective as response prevention in the hospital (Boersma et al 1976; Roper and Rachman, 1976). This is especially important in light of the impracticability of hospitalizing large numbers of obsessive patients for constant supervision.

With the amelioration in obsessive symptoms a subsequent attempt should be made to deal with other fears, phobias, and behavioural deficits which are usually associated with the debilitating neurosis, but which often do not improve with a reduction in obsessive symptoms. Assertive training, modelling or any other behavioural therapy and/or psychotherapy judged to be beneficial should be used to achieve this end. For example, the social behaviour of four successfully treated patients took a decidedly negative turn after therapy (as in the case of a civil servant who, incapacitated before therapy, refused to work though he had recovered and made every attempt to embezzle the government when he recovered). These important changes in the patients' mode of relating to their environment are seldom reflected on the measures generally used to assess outcome. If there are a group of obsessive patients whose psychopathic tendencies become manifest when they are freed from their obsessive symptoms, the treatment program should be modified to include a strategy for increased socialization.

Due to the fluctuations which are common in the course of obsessive neurosis, it is difficult to assess in the absence of a control group how much improvement was due to spontaneous remission or, less likely, symptom substitution. We are now following a fifth group of patients for a period of six months in order to assess the degree of spontaneous remission which occurs in an untreated control group of obsessive neurotics.

A sixth group of obsessive patients is currently under treatment with a "Broad spectrum" behaviour therapy. Because the treatment is tailor-made for each patient, a detailed program outline specifying the target symptoms, the mode of therapeutic intervention, the type of therapies used and their temporal sequence (i.e. concurrent and/or sequential) will be completed for each patient in order to subsequently identify the therapeutic ingredients. With the use of more knowledgeable treatment paradigms and a broadening of our therapeutic goals, we hope to enhance the prognosis of this difficult neurotic disorder.

SUMMARY

Thirty three chronically ill multi-symptomatic obsessive neurotic patients, matched on age, sex, degree of education and duration of illness, received 50 sessions of aversion relief, flooding, thought stopping, or a combination of systematic desensitization and thought stopping. The relative effectiveness of these treatment techniques on each of the four cardinal symptoms of obsessive neurosis was assessed. No pre-selection of treatment was made on the basis of the type of severity of the presenting obsessive-compulsive symptomatology and assignment of patients to the treatment groups was random. Frequency and severity of each of the obsessive symptom clusters, other neurotic symptoms, adjustment in five areas of social functioning, as well as overall anxiety level, number of fears and obsessive traits were assessed before and after treatment. Psychiatrist's ratings and patients' own self-ratings on comprehensive standardized questionnaires as well as psychometric test scores were used to evaluate improvement. The results showed that flooding and thought stopping were most effective overall in reducing the obsessive-compulsive symptomatology (by 50%) on all the assessment measures. A sequential application of a combination of systematic desensitisation and thought stopping was less effective than thought stopping alone. Aversion relief was ineffective, reducing the obsessive-compulsive symptomatology by a clinically insignificant 5%. The obsessive symptom clusters tended to show a differential response to treatment: ruminations and horrific temptations improved most when treated with flooding; rituals were most effectively reduced by thought stopping. There was no significant relationship in degree of improvement among the obsessive symptom clusters and little generalization to other neurotic symptoms, such as phobias. More than half the patients have been reassessed at six and one year after treatment and the improvement is maintained. The results underlined the need for a broad spectrum approach to the treatment of obsessive neurosis, which would involve the joint application of those techniques most effective in treating each of the presenting obsessive-compulsive symptom clusters, and other neurotic symptoms.

REFERENCES:

Akhtar, S., Wig, N.N., Varma, S.K., D. Pershad, and Verma, S.K. (1975). A phenomenological analysis in obsessive-compulsive neurosis. British Journal of Psychiatry, 127, 342-348.

Beech, H.R. (1971). Ritualistic activity in obsessional patients. Journal of Psychosomatic Research, 15, 417-422.

Boersma, K. Den Hengst, S., Dekker, J. and Emmelkamp P.M.G., (1976). Exposure and response prevention in the natural environment. A comparison with obsessive-compulsive patients. Behaviour Research and Therapy, 14, 19-24.

Cooper, J. (1970). The Leyton obsessional inventory. Psychological Medicine, 1, 48-64.

Furst, J.B. and Cooper, A. (1970). Failure of systematic desensitisation in two cases of obsessional-compulsive neurosis marked by fears of insecticide. Behaviour Research and Therapy, 8, 203-206.

Marks, I.M., Hodgson, R. and Rachman, S. (1975). Treatment of chronic obsessive-compulsive neurosis by in-vivo exposure: A two year follow-up and issues in treatment. British Journal of Psychiatry, 127, 349-364.

Meyer, V., Levy, R., and Schnurer, A., (1974). The behavioural treatment of obsessive-compulsive disorders. In Obsessive States (edited by H.R. Beech), London: Methuen and Co. Ltd.

Pujol, R., and Savy, A. (1968). Le Devinir de l' Obsede, p. 17. Marseille: Masson et Cie Editeurs. (Rapport de psychiatrie presente au congres de psychiatrie et de neurologie de langue francaise, Clermont-Ferrand, 1968).

Rachman, S., Hodgson, R. and Marks, I.M. (1971). Treatment of chronic obsessive-compulsive neurosis. Behaviour Research and Therapy 9, 237-247.

Reed, A.F., (1968). Some formal qualities of obsessional thinking. <u>Psychia-tria Clinica</u>, 1, 382–392.

Roper, G. and Rachman, S. (1976). Obsessional-compulsive checking: Experimental replication and development. <u>Behaviour Research and Therapy</u>, 14, 25–32.

Solyom, L., Zamanzadeh, D., Ledwidge, B. and Kenny, F. (1971). Aversion relief treatment of obsessive neurosis. In <u>Advances in Behaviour Therapy</u>, (edited by R. D. Rubin), London: Academic Press.

Stern, R., (1970). Treatment of a case of obsessional neurosis using thought-stopping technique. <u>British Journal of Psychiatry</u>, 117, 441–442.

Straus, E., (1948). On Obsession: A clinical and methodological study. <u>Nervous and Mental Disorders Monograph No</u>. 73.

Walton D., and Mather, M.D., (1963). The application of learning principles to the treatment of obsessive-compulsive states in the acute and chronic phases of illness. <u>Behaviour Research and Therapy</u>, 1, 163–174.

Wolpe, J., and Lang, P.J., (1964). A fear survey schedule for use in behaviour viour therapy. <u>Behaviour Research and Therapy</u>, 2, 27–30.

APPENDIX
AN ILLUSTRATIVE CASE HISTORY FOR EACH
TREATMENT GROUP

Aversion relief

This 54-year old housewife had been obsessive and phobic for 28 years. Her
main symptoms consisted of a ritual house cleaning, which compelled her to
work continuously with a Bissel carpet sweeper in order to erase the tracks
her feet made on the carpet. She tried to avoid this house-cleaning ritual
by spending most of her time in the bathroom, where she also slept. In
addition, she had blasphemous thoughts during church services, feared crowded elevators, and animals. Her scores on the IPAT Anxiety Scale, Fear
Survey Schedule, and the Leyton Symptom and Interference scores were maximum.
Aversion relief was applied in-vivo (in her home), as well as to taped
narratives of her obsessive and phobic experiences. At termination of treatment there was a substantial decrease in her obsessiveness and an almost
complete elimination of the more debilitating phobias. Symptom and interference scores on the Leyton were reduced by half, but there was almost
no change in her anxiety level.

Flooding

A 37-year old housewife and mother of four children experienced her first
obsessive symptom at the age of 21. At the age of 32 her obsessions gradually became cripling and she had to be hospitalized. On admission she
was constantly ruminating, repeating sentences she had heard and asking
herself trivial questions. She was chronically indecisive. She was also
a compulsive hand washer and had a very detailed bathroom ritual which she
followed daily. Her fear that she may have touched Javex, paint, or tur-
pentine completely incapacitated her. She was treated with flooding in
imagination and in-vivo, improved greatly, and was able to resume a normal
productive life-style, for the first time in many years.

Thought stopping

This 43 year-old teacher suffered from all four types of obsessive symptoms,
each of maximum severity. He was constantly ruminative, his many obsessive
thoughts severely interfering with all his work and leisure activities and
preventing him from falling asleep. He feared possession by the devil,
had many horrific temptations, and all-pervading doubt. He had so many
rituals that his entire day was spent in ritualized prayer, walking in
patterns, checking, etc. He was highly anxious even when not concerned
about any of his obsessive symptoms. A numerous course of ECTs and psychotherapy had produced only temporary improvement. As a result of thought
stopping his symptom score was reduced by 50% and his interference score
on the Leyton dropped from a high 62 to 19. He was markedly less rituali-

stic and his ruminations were substantially decreased in frequency and
intensity.

Systematic desensitisation and thought stopping

A 26-year old engineer suffered mostly from obsessive fears of aggressive
intent, both self- and other-directed, which he attempted to mitigate by
ritualistic behaviour, while shaving, using knives, etc.   His anxiety
as measured by the IPAT and psychiatrist's rating was maximum and he had
very high symptom, resistance, and interference scores on the Leyton.
At termination of treatment, his anxiety was only moderately reduced, but
his obsessive fears and associated rituals were reduced by 50% in intensity and frequency and he was able to return to work.

11. BEHAVIOURAL APPROACHES TO OBSESSIVE-COMPULSIVE NEUROSIS

Ron Ramsay

Department of Clinical Psychology, University of Amsterdam, Holland

Some Characteristics of obsessive-compulsives

Most people can recognize in themselves and in others minor habits and rituals which are, to a large extent, senseless, yet when the ritual is disturbed there is a feeling of discomfort. Obsessive-compulsive acts can range from innocent trivialities, through various habits which most people would agree are desirable for making life easier, to intensely strong, persistent and pervasive habits which go far beyond what would be considered reasonable. The amount of subjective discomfort, experienced when such habits are disrupted, can also vary in intensity from mild, momentary uneasiness to violent and long-lasting panic. Thus, there is variation in the number and pervasiveness of habits, and the degree of discomfort when these habits are interrupted.

In most European languages there is just one word to describe these acts, while in English there are two words which attempt to distinguish the cognitive from the motor aspects. This distinction seems to be important at present, as can be seen in the papers written by the Maudsley Group. However, some clinicians claim that there are never obsessions (cognitive) without some motor component (compulsion), and so for treatment purposes this distinction is irrelevant. We will leave the question open for further research to decide. In the discussion at the Symposium, R. Hodgson stated, and most people agreed with him, that "washers" are easier to treat than "checkers". At the moment there is at least a practical therapeutic distinction between obsession and compulsion.

Differences in the pervasiveness of compulsive acts has led some clinicians to try and distinguish between obsessive-compulsive character and neurosis. The former person displays many of these habits in a mild form, in many areas of life, while the latter may have one or more habits which dominate and disrupt completely any reasonable way of life. This distinction between character and neurosis has not been generally accepted; its usefulness has still to be demonstrated.

In general, obsessive-compulsives, are found to score highly on questionnaire measures of neuroticism, indicating that they are emotionally labile and tend towards long periods of high arousal. This personality factor, according to Eysenck's theory, is genetically determined. Whenever there is high arousal there is the tendency to a narrowing of the span of attention, which may be one factor to explain, at least in part, the obsessive-compulsive's focus on one aspect of the environment. Distinction and differentiation between safe and unsafe breaks down under high levels of arousal, the person sees all situations as unsafe, or at least potentially so.

Attempts to find out what precisely the obsessive-compulsive is afraid of usually fail. When minutely questioned, he most often comes up with the answer that there is a feeling that something terrible will happen to him or his family in the future if the rituals are not carried out. What this "some--thing" is, usually remains vague. In past years when religious beliefs were prominent, it often came down to a fear of retribution from God. Now, when religion is less powerful in Western cultures, the fear is more for aggression, accidents, death, or the carrying out of forbidden sexual acts. This aspect of constantly expecting something terrible to heppen led Dr. Victor Meyer in an early paper (1966), to advocate that therapy be directed towards changing the expectations of the client but he has since dropped this approach. Expectations are too difficult to unearth and manipulate, and one can never completely eliminate by cognitive means this dread of something in the future.

Another feature of the obsessive-compulsive deserves mention. Fear of loss of control. If there were little order or certainty in life, we would all find it very difficult to survive, but the obsessive-compulsive seems to need structure and rigidity more than most. He has to keep an iron fist around his feelings, never being able to "let go"; spontaneity is absent, all ingoing and outgoing stimuli have to be carefully checked, filtered and censored, and only then allowed to pass. Have you ever known an obsessive-compulsive to enjoy getting drunk? Control is also invariably extended to the immediate environment, so that family are close friends are included and forced into the ritualistic patterns. Thus the compulsions are not only directed internally towarss the client's thoughts and behaviour, but also externally to others - the client compels others to conform the neurosis.

Coupled with the fear of loss of control is the feeling of uncertainty. In spite of the stringent control clients try to wield over themselves and the environment, they are constantly in doubt about the effectiveness of this, which, of course, leads to renewed ritualistic behaviour plus repetitious asking for reassurance from others. It is probably this characteristic that makes these people so resistant to any form of medication. They resist the effects of a drug, which takes more effort in control and the net result is that they become more, not less anxious.

To end this discussion of some characteristics of obsessive-compulsives, it is worthwhile to bear in mind some of Eysenck's early work on the classifica-tion and diagnosis of psychiatric syndromes. Eysenck (1962, p. 15-16) makes reference to a study which shows obsessive-compulsives to be not only high on neuroticism but also relatively high on psychoticism. This factor of high psychoticism is to my mind important, but has been largely ignored up till now. Rachman (1971) makes the point that ruminations are likely to have a much larger endogenous element than phobic stimuli. We would contend that the endogenous element is paramount. There are trigger elements in the environment, but they are stimuli which most people avoid, and are pro-bably more in the form of "convenience stimuli" on which to hang toe endoge-nous anxiety. Where we then take techniques which have been developed for the treatment of neurotic hehaviour and apply these to a syndrome in which psychotic elements are prominent, we can expect to run into difficulties.

Behaviour therapy approaches

In the field of 'mental illness" the broadest diagnosiic categorization is into that of neurosis and psychosis. The obsessive-compulsive syndrome is usually regarded as a neurosis and has proved to be the most intractible and distres-sing of all the various neurotic subdivisions.

From about 1960 onwards behaviour therapy gained momentum in the treatment of various neurotic complaints, and after an initial burst of wild enthusiasm, settled down to the long, hard task of evaluating itself - what are the active ingredients in a therapeutic package, are the good results standing up over time, what treatment, by whom, is most effective for a particular individual with a specific problem, under which set of circumstances, and how does it come about (Paul, 1969). In the early years of behaviour therapy the burgeoning literature contained little reference to the treatment of obsessive-compulsives. A comprehensive reference list (Peck, Bradshaw and Ashcroft) covering the 10 years 1960 to 1969 contains more than 1300 studies, of which only 10 refer to obsessive-compulsives. This almost negation of an important neurotic problem probably does not mean that behaviour therapists were not interested, but more likely that they were not getting good results. Failures are either not written up or articles containing no positive results are excluded from publication.

Since 1970 there has been an upsurge in the number of behaviour therapy articles devoted to the theory and treatment of obsessive-compulsive neurosis. In the English Journal Behaviour Research and Therapy there appear 6 articles in the years 1971-73. (In the American journal of Behaviour Therapy, there is 1 for those years). At the first European Association for Behaviour Therapy in Munich, 1971, two papers were devoted to obsessive-compulsives, and now the topic has a regular place in the annual congresses, with panel discussions, free papers, and workshops. At the first International Symposium on Behaviour Modification in Minneapolis, Minnesota, in 1972 and at the sixth A.A.B.T. congress in New York in 1972, the topic of behaviour therapy for obsessive-compulsives was not even mentioned. It is possibly appropriate here to give credit to the small group of English therapists for pioneering the treatment methods which show such promise, and for stimulating others to take up the challenge in this field to that Western Europe seems to be leading the way for the rest of the world. (See Rachman, Hodgson and Marzillier, 1970; Rachman, Hodgson and Marks, 1971; Hodgson and Rachman, 1972; Rachman, Marks and Hodgson, 1973; Roper, Rachman and Hodgson, 1973; Roper, Rachman and Marks, 1975; Roper and Rachman, 1976.

It is interesting to speculate on what the relationship will be between theory and research in this area. Theories abound, but they are difficult to verify or falsify, and it is difficult to devise analogue studies of obsessive-compulsive neurosis in the laboratory. Now that we have methods for breaking down such behaviour in the natural conditions in which it occurs, we have in principle ways of manipulating conditions which would affect the maintenance, maybe even the development of such behaviours. Thus we have the opportunity of, via a systematic approach to therapy, throwing light on the theory of compulsions.

It may seem out of place in a book on behaviour therapy to bring in the topic of psycho-surgery. However, there are indications in the literature that, although the results of this drastic treatment are mixed, when the effects on compulsives are looked at separately, the picture is not so cloudy. There is some evidence that, for intractible cases where all else fails, psycho-surgery followed by behaviour therapy can produce results. It would be wise then, even though we have not included an article in this reader, for behaviour therapists to keep up in the literature in this area, expecially as recent developments, such as electrode implantation, look so promising.

REFERENCES:

Eysenck, H.J. (1961). Classification and the problem of diagnosis. In H. J. Eysenck (Ed.) Handbook of Abnormal Psychology, New York, Basic Books.

Hodgson, R. J. and S. Rachman (1972). The effects of contamination and washing in obsessional patients. Behaviour Research and Therapy, 10, 111-117.

Meyer, V. (1966). Modification of expectations in cases with obsessional rituals. Behaviour Modification Therapy, 4, 273-280.

Paul, G. (1969). Behaviour Modification Research: design and tactics. In C.N. Franks (Ed.) Behaviour Therapy: appraisal and status. New York, McGraw Hill.

Peck, D.F., Bradshaw, P.W. and Ashcroft, J.B. Reference list for Behaviour Therapy Literature, London: The British Psychological Society.

Rachman, S. (1971). Obsessional ruminations. Behaviour Research and Therapy, 9, 229-236,

Rachman, S., Hodgson, R. and Marzillier, J. (1970). Treatment of an obsessional-compulsive disorder by modelling. Behaviour Research and Therapy, 8, 385-392.

Rachman, S., Hodgson, R. and Marks, I.M. (1971). The treatment of chronic obsessive-compulsive neurosis. Behaviour Research and Therapy, 9, 237-248.

Rachman, S., Marks, I.M., and Hodgson R., (1973). The treatment of obsessive-compulsive neurotics by modelling and flooding in-vivo. Behaviour Research and Therapy, 11, 463-472.

Roper, G., Rachman, S., and Hodgson R., A, experiment on obsessional checking. Behaviour Research and therapy, 11, 271-278.

Roper, G. and Rachman S., and Marks I.M. (1975). Passive and participant modelling in exposure treatment of obsessive-compulsive neurotics, Behaviour Research and Therapy, 13, 291-280.

Roper G., and Rachman, S. (1976). Obsessional-compulsive checking: experimental replication and development. Behaviour Research and Therapy, 14, 25-32.

12. TREATMENT OF OBSESSIONS, COMPULSIONS AND PHOBIAS AS HIDDEN COUPLE - COUNSELING

Iver Hand, Brigitte Spoehring and Edda Stanik

Psychiatric Clinic, University of Hamburg, W. Germany

Introduction

It has now become commonplace that psychological problems - usually called 'neurotic symptoms' - occur in a social microsystem and not only in the sick individual, the patient. Yet, in many cases, individual treatment of circumscribed problems like compulsions or phobias remains the most sensible form of help. If the patient learns to give up, reduce or cope with one particular set of problems he may become able to tackle others in a similar way, including those in human relationships. Generalization may be enhanced if specific treatments include management of general anxiety/depression and training in problem solving. Nevertheless, when patients with obsessions and compulsions or phobias suffer simultaneously from marital discord, a purely "symptom" - directed approach may not be sufficient. Behaviour therapy literature usually does not mention the frequency, function or relevance for treatment-outcome of marital discord in patients who have received symptom-treatment. Some of the reports which refer to this topic give contradictory views (Emmelkamp 1977; Goldstein 1971; Hafner and Marks 1976; Hand and Lamontagne 1976; Lazarus 1971; Liotti and Guidano 1976; Schaper 1971). There is also a lack of controlled investigations about how successful symptom-treatment affects relationships. Thus, it is difficult to deduce possible interactions between a symptom and relationship problems. From a social systems approach symptoms are supposed to have an instrumental function in relationships, but the current state of research in psychotherapy does not allow reliable predictions as to what it is best to do under particular conditions, when a patient with compulsions or phobias lives in a disturbed interpersonal setting. A basic methodological problem must be solved regarding the measurement of marital discord in couples where symptoms have a protective function i.e. the couple's ratings about their marriage would always be positive. Successful symptom-treatment can have manifold, though hardly predictable effects on "good" and "bad" relationships (Hand and Lamontagne 1976). The same seems to apply to unsuccessful symptom-treatment. When marital discord is evident, with certain patients the therapists' incentive to undertake couple-counseling is much stronger than the couple's willingness to receive it. We find ourselves in such a position whenever assessment interviews give the impression that phobic or obsessional symptoms are indeed symptomatic of a disturbed relationship - whether the symptoms are caused by or are simply maintained for this reason.

We agree with Marks that, generally the label "symptom" should not be used to differentiate phobias or obsessions from relationship "problems", since this would suggest that these are always two entirely different classes of illness. The term "symptom" is used in the following because, for the particular couple involved, we had the impression that their obsessions, compulsions and phobias were symptomatic of their marital discord.

One way of predisposing such couples, for relationship-counseling is first
to satisfy their wish for more symptom-treatment. If this fails, the couple
may reach such a crisis that both partners come to want to improve their
relationship. An example of successful contract therapy, after failure of
individual behavioural treatment with an obsessive-compulsive patient, has
been published by Stern and Marks (1973).

Obviously a different approach is necessary for a second type of couples when,
after symptom-treatment, only one partner wants contract therapy while the
other refuses it.

Further there is a third type of couples where both partners deny the existen-
ce of or refuse help for their relationship problems, in spite of long-lasting
and treatment-resistant symptoms that make them suffer. For these patients
the treatment approach proposed here has been disigned. Essentially it
means doing couple-counseling without naming it, in the context of symptom-
therapy.

The treatment hypothesis

Behaviour therapy literature about phobics and obsessive-compulsives, as well
as general clinical experience, gives the impression that patients' spouses
quite readily accept the role of a co-therapist in individual symptom-treatment (Marks 1975; Mathews, Teasdale, Munby, Johnston and Shaw, 1976). If
patients and their spouses in type three couples are prepared to do the same
then it would seem promising to try and change their symptom-centered "patient-
cotherapist" interaction into exercises concerning their general interaction,
both then having a "patient"-role. This would have to be done in a way that
the couple does not consciously realize the shift from the symptom-level to
the relationship-level, as otherwise they would probably drop out of treatment.
This strategy may well be possible, because such couples complain about a lot
of concrete difficulties in their daily life - and they regard these as due
to the symptom, not to a disturbed relationship. If the therapist does not
argue about their theory, he can still work with the basic problems on the
practical level. This appears to be a legitimate way to use paradoxical
communication. Such an approach is the reverse of what Stern and Marks described above with a "type one" couple.

So far we have completed one treatment of this kind, including a six months
follow-up. Systematic research into this area is under way.

The couple

The couple had been married for twenty years when the 48 years old husband
came for treatment of his obsessions and compulsions. One complaint was the
ruminations which he had first experienced shortly after he became engaged
to his wife. They consisted of aggressive thoughts against her.

Three years after their wedding, when their only son had been born, his
thoughts turned against his son and remained so with varying intensities until the son died in 1972, then aged 17. Later his thoughts increased to an
unbearable extent at home as well as at work. He now labelled them "bad
thoughts", as he could not stop thinking "how nice that our son is dead".
At the same time this caused severe feelings of guilt. His wife on the other

hand had shown a continuous grief reaction after the death of the son, and took this as a reason for not engaging in any pleasurable activity, neither alone nor with her husband. These two responses to their son's death seemed to have become quite independent from their original cause, now being used by the couple to fight each other.

A second problem of the husband was his insistance on extreme cleanness and orderliness in their home, where his wife on the other hand had always been proud of her qualities as a house wife. The couple did not fight openly about this question, but frustrated each other indirectly in many subtle ways. He would control a number of items when coming home, pretending not to do so; she would always try to do things 101% so as to give him no chance to make her feel humiliated.

A third problem of the husband was his checking ritual at work. His working ability had always been impaired by an inferiority complex and varying self-imposed checking rituals, according to the specific conditions of his work. At the time of this treatment, he was spending up to four hours checking rather than working and he was again worried that he would loose his job.

Over the years several treatment measures (hypnosis, medication) had shown little or no effect. Only a psychoanalysis over three years, some 15 years ago, had helped him to give up a specific checking ritual at work, gain more self-confidence and eventually get a better job. Ruminations and marital discord had remained unchanged. He stopped his analysis when it had led to a point where changes in his marriage seemed unavoidable. He had a first relapse when his company went bankrupt some 6 years ago and further deterioration began after his son died.

The wife had suffered from agoraphobia ever since their engagement. Several treatment attempts (including 3 years of psychoanalytic group therapy) had little or no effect. When our treatment started she was able to walk only very short distances on her own, after having taken tranquillizers.

For the 1.5 years before this treatment started the couple had not had sexual intercourse because of the husband's psychogenic impotence. This was another field of continuous mutual indirect attacks. The husband seemed convinced that he had married his wife only because he "felt sorry" for her due to her unattractiveness.

Therapists' treatment aims and treatment package

After an individual as well as a joint interview had shown that there was no way of getting the couple to accept direct marital therapy, we offered treatment for the husband's complaints with the wife as co-therapist. Additionally the wife was to get some advice how to overcome her agoraphobia.

We decided to direct the symptom-treatment at the "bad thoughts" and the controlling-behaviour at home, as both seemed directly connected with their general interaction problems. Our hypothesis was that, if this symptom-treatment could be turned into hidden marital counseling, then any success in this area should extend to the symptoms at work. To test this assumption, no direct treatment was to be given for the checking ritual.

The "treatment-package"

1.   Symptom-specific techniques:
     a)   "acting out" of ruminations (bad thoughts) during treatment sessions.
     b)   symptom-prescription for control-behaviour in the home and for
          ruminations, both as part of their home work.
     c)   Change of the patient's labelling of his ruminations as "bad thoughts"
          into "specific thoughts".

2.   "Hidden" couple-counseling:
     a)   Structured communication about symptom-related topics of discord
          like control-behaviour and standards of cleanness in the home, i.e.
          "symptom-centered interactional retraining" as one specific aspect
          of problem solving skills.
     b)   Contract exercises for mutual positive reinforcements (Azrin and
          Naster 1973; Liberman 1975; Stuart 1975).
     c)   Structured exercises in open communication of feelings, at the begin-
          ning of treatment only during the occurance of the symptoms (see
          "executive sessions" Liberman 1975).
     d)   Assertive training, including strategies to gain independence from
          the husband's family.
     e)   Advice in line with the early stages of the Masters and Johnson pro-
          gramme, consisting of prohibition of sexual intercourse, and pres-
          cription of cuddling exercises not involving the genital area.

This package of strategies was administered in five successive phases, in 7
sessions of individual symptom-treatments for the husband and 32 joint sessions with the couple. Total treatment time was 87 hours, spread over 6
months, as compared to 6.5 years of individual and group psychoanalysis which
both had in the past.

Treatment process and effects

Phase one: Symptom-treatment with the obsessive-compulsive husband. He had
4 sessions during 1.5 weeks period. Three of the four sessions consisted mainly of "acting out" of the ruminations. The most remarkable event during this
phase occured in the first session, when the patient while hammering at a
cushion and shouting thoughts against his son, suddenly turned the aggressive-
ness against his wife. After a very brief break of surprise he went on in
this way until he reached a state of physical and emotional exhaustion. This
seemed to confirm our pre-treatment hypothesis about the function of these
ruminations in the relationship. Outside these particular exercises the
husband did not admit aggressive feelings against his wife although he beha-
ved increasingly aggressively in a direct way. The therapists did nothing
to confront him with the marital problem any further than this spontaneous
process initiated during the first three sessions. The "bad thoughts" were
labelled as "specific thoughts" to make the exercise easier to accept by the
patient. In between sessions the patient was given home work mainly as
symptom-prescription, i.e. he had to repeat any spontaneously occuring rumination at least five times in order to interrupt his usual response chain.

During this phase the patient recorded a decrease in ruminations and an increase in tension at home. He became worried about the marriage. The wife
had stopped taking tranquilizers and had made a considerable improvement in

her agoraphobia, with very little advice on how to apply graded exposure in vivo.

Phase two: "Hidden" couple-counseling (exercises a-d). One individual and 8 joint sessions with the couple during 4 weeks period.

The co-therapist function of the wife was easily accepted by both. The joint sessions and the in between (tape-recorded) home work consisted mainly of training in structured communication (norm-finding about cleanness and order-liness) about the symptoms at home. Because of the nature of the symptom this led quickly to dealing with the real feelings towards each other and allowed us to add structured exercises in open communication. Further, we introduced the exchange of small positive reinforcements in daily life activities. Another long lasting reason for mutual indirect attacks, i.e. how to gain more independence from the husband's family, was dealt with by assertive training and problem-solving techniques. Additionally the wife was given further instructions regarding her agoraphobia. Both were cooperative in all sessions.

At the end of phase two both felt their living together was much improved. The husband continued feeling definitely improved in his ruminations and also in the symptoms at home. The couple went on a holiday after having received intensive "behaviour rehearsal" regarding rules to follow during holiday. It turned out to be a honeymoon, "our best time ever". But the husband had a relapse in his ruminations and he did not apply the symptom-prescription.

Phase three: Continuation of phase two exercises, now including sexual thera-py. One individual and 12 joint sessions during 7 weeks period.

The relapse in the ruminations was quickly overcome by using again symptom-prescription. Newly introduced were an assertive training for their general social anxiety and the early exercises of a modified Masters and Johnson programme for their sexual problem. During the latter, intercourse being prohibited, the couple had one "accidental" but successful intercourse which they "could not believe" afterwards. It was followed by an immediate increa-se in obsessive-compulsive symptoms. This might be interpreted as a signal that the sexual improvement - like the early rapid improvement in the rumi-nations and home-related symptoms - was threatening as it was much faster than the improvement of the emotional side of their relationship.

The relapse did not show a continuous pattern, but rather an increase (Fig 12.2) in "relapse-spikes". These seemed to depend more on previous distress at home than on stress at work. In spite of them, the husband reported an increase in satisfaction at work and a remarkable overall decrease in symptoms. He also started reducing his psychopharmacological medication.

Phase four: Intensified attempt of the therapists to leave the symptom level and treat the relationship directly. Offer of marital therapy. Ten joint sessions during 6 weeks period.

The wife refused to continue the structured dialogue about the symptoms concerning the home. Both had had to express dissatisfaction openly whenever they felt it while the symptom occured. The husband used this "right" in a way that the wife felt attacked on a general, not just the household, level.

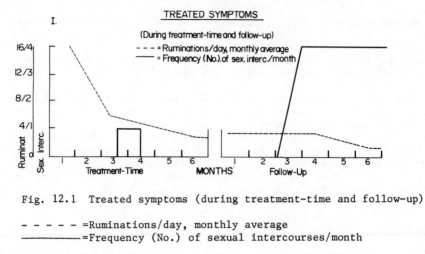

Fig. 12.1   Treated symptoms (during treatment-time and follow-up)

- - - - - =Ruminations/day, monthly average
─────────=Frequency (No.) of sexual intercourses/month

She insisted that this was distrust rather than criticism, and she no longer accepted it as one of his illness-behaviours.   She got scared about the future of their marriage and felt "paralyzed".

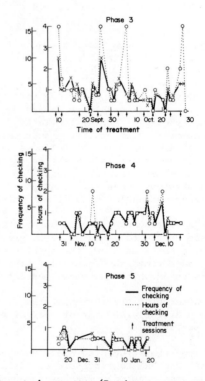

Fig. 12.2   Untreated symptom (During treatment-time)

At this point both experienced intensive separation anxiety. They could talk about it openly and made a contract without the therapists, which did not allow him any further critical or aggressive remarks during the exercises at home, but only in the meetings with the therapists.

The therapists made another attempt to motivate the couple for a frankly accepted marital counseling. This was refused mainly by the wife who insisted that the marriage was good and that they only needed some more help for his symptoms.

The checking at work was reduced by about fifty percent as compared to that in phase three. The specific thoughts and the symptoms in the home were also reduced further. The wife's agoraphobia was much improved. During phase four, the couple had had a second "accidental" sexual intercourse following one of the prescribed cuddling-exercises which at this point, still excluded the genitals. This time the couple did believe it and responded with happiness rather than symptoms.

Phase five: Separation from therapists. One individual and 2 joint sessions during 4 weeks period.

The husband had agreed with his wife in the last joint interview but tried to get a coalition with the therapists in a subsequent individual session which he had requested. The therapists adopted a "Colombo" strategy, telling the couple that they had no power to do any more for the remaining symptoms and that all ought to be happy if there were no marital problems for which they could offer some help.

For the first time the couple became aggressive with the therapists, accusing them of incompetence and inability to solve difficult problems. Both made clear they would do the remaining work on their own.

Surprisingly, in a subsequent final joint session the couple agreed with the termination of treatment, in a friendly way, expressing satisfaction with the goal achieved.

The symptoms were further reduced. Checking at work had decreased to a negligible extent. The ruminations occured even less than in phase four. The symptoms in the home had nearly disappeared. The wife's agoraphobia remained much improved. The general interaction had been constantly more rewarding. The husband felt that he had learned that his criticism was really his own problem and he had begun to open up to his wife more trustfully. The only severe disturbance left was the sexual problem. Also both wanted still more independence from his family.

Four months' follow-up

The couple appeared to be very happy at their first follow-up. The checking rituals were down nearly to zero. The ruminations still occured 2-3 times a day, briefly without really bothering the husband. The home-related symptoms had completely disappeared, which the husband felt was due to his insight and his acceptance that his wife's standards were different from those of his mother.

The psychogenic impotence had dramatically improved during the last four
weeks before the follow-up, the couple now having intercourse once a week.
They felt, this had been due to their continuation of the prescribed fondling
exercises. Their daily life interaction was much improved. Both had developed a number of joint activities and regarded their living together as much
more rewarding than at any time before this treatment.

The wife had completely lost her agoraphobia, she had never used tranquillizers since phase two. The husband had reduced his medication to fifty percent of the original dosage.

Six months' follow-up

The ruminations were further reduced and now did not bother the husband at
all. The checking rituals could not be judged as the couple had just come
back from another honeymoon-holiday. The wife's agoraphobia remained cured.
Sex life had improved even more, as both could now openly discuss their
wishes and feelings in this area and continued to enjoy intercourse once a
week. Both also regarded the relationship as further improved, both being
in a better mood than at the previous follow-up.

They still wanted more independence from his family, but appeared confident
in this respect.

Discussion

We feel that we were able to follow the treatment design and that the effects
were in the anticipated direction. Unfortunately, treatment process and
outcome are documented inadequately as far as "hard" data are concerned.
Except for sexual behaviour there is also no pre-treatment baseline. Work
with this kind of couple now uses standardized ratings for symptoms, emotions
and interaction patterns.

This research uses the whole treatment-package as we feel each of the components was important. The relative impact of the single ingredients might
be investigated if future results with the whole package are as encouraging
as in this pilot-treatment.

The objective evaluation has been tried from the second and third phase of
therapy. It was only possible to get the husband to do "average estimates"
for intervals of from one week to one month, but they seem sufficient to show
changes in the treated and untreated symptoms (Figs. 12.1 and 12.2). There
are no such ratings about the wife's symptom and the interactional patterns
of the couple.

The narrative evaluation has been in an unusually detailed manner, not only
to make up for the lack of "hard" data, but also to encourage replications.

We hesitate to discuss possible mechanisms on the background of these data.
The following are tentative suggestions about what might have happened. The
treatment may have confronted the couple in a sort of successive approximation, via symptom-centered exercises, with the disrupted parts of their
relationship. But this the symptoms may have lost their protective function.
At this point (phase four) the couple broke the contract with the therapists

and created their home-made solution which only allowed them to be nice with each other. The symptoms no longer were a safeguard against painful confrontation with each others' real feelings. If this had been the only effect, i.e. scaring them into a compromise, lasting benefits would seem most unlikely, even for the six months' follow-up. The couple may therefore additionally have become stimulated to apply at their own speed during follow-up, the techniques and skills learned during treatment. This seems to be supported by the continuing improvement during follow-up showing itself most clearly in their sexual behaviour.

The couple quit treatment when open emphasis was put on marital counseling - at the same point when the husband had quit his previous psychoanalysis. The difference of this couple-oriented behavioural approach seems to lie in the follow-up effects, the stability of which still remains to be shown.

REFERENCES:

Azrin, N., Naster B., (1973). Reciprocity counceling. Behaviour Research and Therapy, 11, 365-382.

Emmelkamp P., (1977). Phobias - theoretical and behavioural treatment considerations. In J. C. Boulougouris and A. Rabavilas (Eds.). Phobic and Obsessive-Compulsive Disorders, Pergamon Press, London.

Goldstein A., (1971). Learning theory insufficiency in understanding agoraphobia - a plea for empiricism. Paper presented at the 1st Annual Meeting of the European Association of Behaviour Therapy, Munich.

Hafner J, Marks I. (1976). Exposure in-vivo of agoraphobics: contributions of diazepam, group exposure, and anxiety evocation. Psychological Medicine 6, 71-88.

Hand I., Lamontagne Y., (1976). The exacerbation of interpersonal problems after rapid phobia removal. Psychotherapy: Theory, Research and Practice, In press.

Lazarus A. (1971). Behaviour Therapy and Beyond. Mc Graw Hill, N.Y.

Liberman R., (1975). Married couples workshop. Leader's guide. Unpublished manuscript.

Liotti G., Guidano V., (1976). Behavioural analysis of marital interaction in agoraphobic male patients. Behaviour Research and Therapy, 14, 161-162.

Marks, I.M. (1975). Behavioural treatment of phobic and obsessive-compulsive disorders: a critical appraisal. In M. Hersen, R.M. Eisler and P.M. Miller (Eds.) Progress in Behaviour Modification. Vol. 1, Academic Press, London.

Mathews, A.A., Teasdale J., Munby M., Johnston, D.W., and Shaw, P.M. (1976). A home-based treatment programme for agoraphobia. Unpublished manuscript.

Schaper W. (1971). Some aspects of the interaction between phobias and their partners. Paper presented at the 1st Annual Meeting of the European Association for Behaviour Therapy, Munich.

Stern, R., and Marks, I.M. (1973). Contract therapy in obsessive-compulsive neurosis with marital discord, British Journal of Psychiatry, 123, 681-684.

Stuart, R. S. (1975). Behavioural remedies for marital ills: a guide to the use of operant-interpersonal techniques. In Thompson, T. and Dockens, W. S. (Eds.) Applications of Behaviour Modification.   Academic Press, New York.

13. SYNCHRONY AND CONCORDANCE ON SUBJECTIVE AND PSYCHOPHYSIOLOGICAL MEASURES AFTER BETA-BLOCKADE AND FLOODING IN OBSESSIVE-COMPULSIVE PATIENTS

Andreas Rabavilas, John Boulougouris and Costas Stefanis

Eginition Hospital, Department of Psychiatry, Athens University

INTRODUCTION

Rachman and Hodgson (1974) in a review of literature concerning psychophysiological responses and behaviour modification of avoidance in humans together with data from animal experiments, concluded that, at times, changes in fear and avoidance could co-vary or vary independently or even inversely. The term "synchrony" was employed to describe the former condition while, where the fear varied independently or inversely with avoidance, the concept of "desynchrony" was introduced. In view of the suggestion that emotions could be expressed through multiple response systems (Lang 1971), it was proposed that the relationship between these systems was of importance and the terms "concordance" and "discordance" were introduced to indicate whether this relationship had a high (concordance) or low (discordance) correlational value. Since the notions of synchrony and concordance were introduced, certain hypotheses were proposed regarding their practical and theoretical implications (Rachman and Hodgson 1974; Hodgson and Rachman 1974). It was suggested that "desynchrony was a function of the intensity of emotional arousal, level of demand, therapeutic technique, length of follow-up and choice of physiological measure" (Hodgson and Rachman 1974). Most literature reviewed by these authors, as a basis for the above hypotheses, concerned findings with phobic patients because data, from physiological investigations of patients exhibiting active avoidance, were not then available. Investigation on these lines would also provide some evidence for or against the two-stage theory (Mowrer 1960; Rachman 1976) which has dominated our psychological thinking over the past decades.

A second line of interest to the present work, concerned the efficacy of flooding as a therapeutic method for obsessive-compulsive disorders. Improvement observed after treatment, although well documented (Marks 1976), was poorly understood, at least in psychophysiological terms, while there was a suggestion (Hodgson and Rachman 1974) that therapeutic change could be related to synchronous changes across several response systems. In terms of psychophysiological responses in obsessive-compulsive patients, skin conductance and subjective anxiety, experienced during the presentation of high affect stimuli, were decreased after flooding (Boulougouris, Rabavilas and Stefanis 1977). Heart rate was resistant to change in such patients whereas in phobic patients it seemed a reliable physiological index of therapeutic change. Such findings necessitate further exploration of the suggestion that skin conductance, in contrast to heart rate, might be a multi-system response loosely paralleling subjective anxiety reports (Lang, Malamed and Hart 1970; Hodgson and Rachman 1974).

Accordingly, the aim of this study was twofold: (a) to examine the psychophysiological and subjective responses in obsessive-compulsive patients to certain testing conditions before and after flooding treatment, in terms of synchrony, and (b) to investigate the synchrony of these response systems after the administration of a pharmaceutical agent having an established effect on one of the psychophysiological parameters employed. A beta-blockade agent (Practolol) was used because previous study had shown that it produced a significant drug effect on heart rate, while changes in skin conductance measures were minimal (Boulougouris, Rabavilas and Stefanis 1975) and no drug effect was recorded on the subjective anxiety ratings.

It was hypothesized that:
1.   After flooding, the synchrony between subjective anxiety and psychophysiological measures will be greater compared to the pre-trial state of after Practolol.
2.   Skin conductance measures will produce higher correlations with subjective anxiety than heart rate after flooding. This hypothesis was based on the assumption that a multi-system response had a greater chance of being affected by such a therapeutic intervention as flooding therapy.
3.   Practolol will produce desynchrony between subjective anxiety and heart rate compared to the pre-trial state or after flooding, while synchrony of skin conductance measures and subjective anxiety will not be affected.
4.   Practolol will reduce correlations between heart rate and other psychophysiological measures.

METHOD

Subjects: Sixteen obsessive-compulsive patients, six female and ten male, with an age range of 20 to 45 years, were studied. Their duration of illness ranged from 6 to 15 years. Patients with depressive, schizophrenic or organic features were not included. Medication was omitted ten days prior to the start of the trial. All patients remained free from psychotropic drugs during the treatment period.

Procedure: The trial was carried out in two stages (Fig. 13.1).

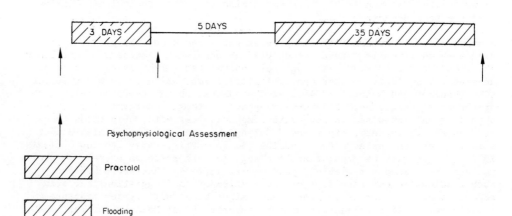

Fig. 13.1 Experimental design

In the first, the patients were under a three-day trial of Practolol, consisting of two daily administrations of 150 mgs of the agent. In the second, the same patients underwent flooding treatment. The latter consisted of ten two-hour sessions, given twice weekly, and included exposures in fantasy and in-vivo of the same duration.

Assessment: All patients had three identical psychophysiological assessments (Fig. 13.2), e.g. baseline, after Practolol and after flooding.

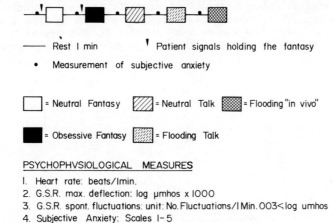

Fig. 13.2. Procedure of psychophysiological assessment.

The following psychophysiological measures were taken:- Skin conductance (Maximum deflection and spontaneous fluctuations), heart rate and subjective anxiety experienced by the patients during the presentation of five kinds of stimuli (i.e. neutral and flooding talk, neutral and obsessive fantasy and flooding "in-vivo" testing conditions of the same duration). These stimuli remained unchanged in all three psychophysiological assessments. A rest followed each testing condition and during this the patients recorded their subjective anxiety regarding the proceding stimulus on a five-point scale.

Recording apparatus and scoring: Skin conductance and heart rate were measured with a Lafayette recorder while the patients were sitting in a quiet, isolated and semi-dark room. For the heart rate, the measure employed was the increase in beats from the maximum 20 sec. count in the rest period to the maximum 20 sec. count during the fantasy, talk or "in-vivo" periods. For the same intervals, measures were taken of fluctuations in skin conductance greater than .003 log micromhos and of maximum deflection of skin conductance calculated in log micromhos x 1000. In order to assess synchrony between the changes of the different measures a reference value was taken as follows:

The overall mean change, from the rest period, of the five testing conditions was calculated after Practolol and after flooding for each variable separately. This score was subtracted from the corresponding changes during the baseline assessment.

RESULTS

The relations of the physiological changes with those in subjective anxiety reports on baseline and after Practolol and flooding are illustrated in **Figs.** 13.3 and 13.4. The greatest proximity of the lines indicates the maximum synchrony.

Before trial, the relationship of subjective anxiety to physiological measures appeared to be minimal during high affect stimuli. Neutral fantasy produces the greatest relationship between these response systems in skin conductance measures, while on heart rate the neutral stimuli did not appear to produce equally high relationship to compare to other physiological measures.

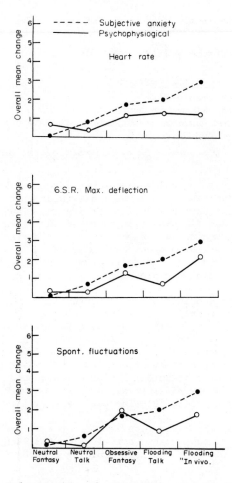

Fig. 13.3 Relationship of subjective anxiety to psychophysiological measures during baseline assessment.

After Practolol, desynchrony between the two response systems appeared to be produced regarding all physiological parameters and in particular spontaneous fluctuations, while such desynchrony was comparatively minimal in skin conductance, maximum deflection (GSR).   Obsessive fantasy and flooding "in-vivo" produced the greatest desynchrony (Fig. 13.4).

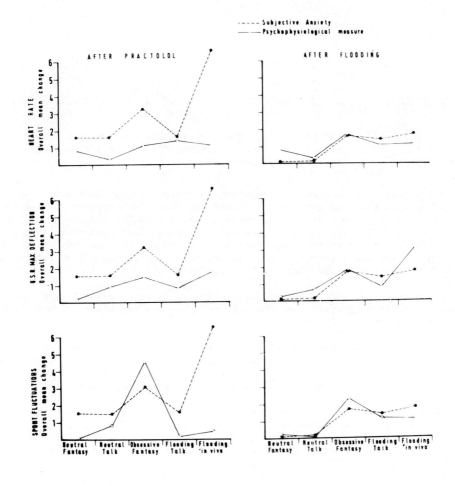

Fig. 13.4   The effects of Practolol and flooding on synchrony
            between psychophysiological measures and subjective
            anxiety during the testing conditions.

On the other hand, desynchrony between the three physiological measures was more evident during obsessive fantasy, while such desynchrony was minimal between GSR measures during the neutral testing conditions (Fig. 13.5).

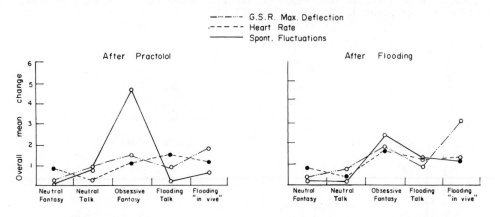

Fig. 13.5   The effects of Practolol and flooding on synchrony between G.S.R. measures and heart rate during the testing conditions.

After flooding, all changes from baseline in the physiological measures showed synchrony with those of subjective anxiety reports.   Such synchrony was more evident in heart rate and G.S.R. maximum deflection during obsessive fantasy with maximum deflection and spontaneous fluctuations during neutral fantasy (Fig. 13.4).   On the other hand, synchrony was evident between changes in all three physiological measures in all testing conditions, with the exception of maximum deflection during flooding "in-vivo" (13.5).

The correlations of subjective anxiety ratings with psychophysiological measures in the testing conditions employed before and after Practolol and flooding are presented in Table 13.1.

Before trial, the greatest correlations were obtained between G.S.R. maximum deflection and subjective anxiety, while heart rate correlated to a lesser degree with subjective anxiety.   Spontaneous fluctuations elicited the lowest correlations.   Higher correlations were obtained during high affect stimuli.

Flooding produced higher trends than Practolol in ten of the fifteen correlations obtained.   During neutral conditions, Practolol elicited higher correlations in spontaneous fluctuations and in G.S.R. maximum deflection during neutral talk.   In contrast, flooding caused higher correlations in heart rate and G.S.R. maximum deflection during neutral fantasy.

During high affect stimuli, flooding resulted in higher correlations, compared to Practolol or to baseline, in G.S.R. maximum deflection in all three high affect testing conditions, in spontaneous fluctuations during obsessive fantasy and flooding talk and in heart rate during flooding "in-vivo". Practolol elicited higher correlations only in heart rate during obsessive fantasy, while in almost all remaining testing conditions the correlations were lower compared to those obtained before trial or after flooding.

SUBJECTIVE ANXIETY

		G.S.R. MAXIMUM DEFLECTION					SPONTANEOUS FLUCTUATIONS					HEART RATE				
		N.F.	N.T.	O.F.	F.T.	F.V.	N.F.	N.T.	O.F.	F.T.	F.V.	N.F.	N.T.	O.F.	F.T.	F.V.
Neutral Fantasy	BT	-.46					.00					.01				
	AP	.29					.33					-.38				
	AF	.50					.20					.77				
Neutral Talk	BT		.01					.00					.00			
	AP		-.53					.75					.65			
	AF		-.37					.002					.90			
Obsessive Fantasy	BT			.57					.30					.32		
	AP			.007					-.25					-.64		
	AF			.72					.55					-.53		
Flooding Talk	BT				.59					-.11					.47	
	AP				.46					.19					.23	
	AF				-.61					-.57					.13	
Flooding "in vivo"	BT					.64					-.29					-.41
	AP					-.06					-.05					.03
	AF					.74					.07					-.58

Table 13.1   Correlations between subjective anxiety and psychophysiological measure on baseline (BT) and after Practolol (AP) and flooding (AF).

The intercorrelations between physiological measures before and after Practolol and flooding are presented in Table 13.2.

Table 13.2   Intercorrelations of pschophysiological measures on baseline (BT) and after Practolol (AP) and flooding (AF)

G.S.R. MAX.DEFLECTION		HEART RATE					SPONTANEOUS FLUCTUATIONS				
		N.F.	N.T.	O.F.	F.T.	F.V.	N.F.	N.T.	O.F.	F.T.	F.V.
Neutral Fantasy	BT	-.36					.32				
	AP	-.91					.17				
	AF	.46					.73				
Neutral Talk	BT		-.48					.15			
	AP		.001					-.31			
	AF		.002					-.37			
Obsessive Fantasy	BT			.01					.81		
	AP			.12					.47		
	AF			-.12					.88		
Flooding Talk	BT				.36					.48	
	AP				.51					.65	
	AF				.42					.68	
Flooding "in vivo"	BT					-.69					-.04
	AP					-.51					.09
	AF					.87					.40

SPONTANEOUS FLUCTUATIONS		HEART RATE				
		N.F.	N.T.	O.F.	F.T.	F.V.
Neutral Fantasy	BT	.40				
	AP	.07				
	AF	.39				
Neutral Talk	BT		.47			
	AP		.37			
	AF		.31			
Obsessive Fantasy	BT			.28		
	AP			.12		
	AF			.05		
Flooding Talk	BT				.44	
	AP				.44	
	AF				.35	
Flooding "in vivo"	BT					.48
	AP					-.13
	AF					-.72

Flooding produced higher correlations compared to baseline or after Practolol between G.S.R. maximum deflection and spontaneous fluctuations in all testing conditions. Higher correlations were obtained between heart rate and maximum deflection after flooding, during flooding "in-vivo", and after Practolol, during neutral fantasy and flooding talk.

DISCUSSION

These findings suggested that flooding facilitated synchrony and concordance between subjective anxiety and physiological measures in obsessive-compulsive patients. High affect stimuli produced concordance between the two response systems under investigation. This agreed with the hypothesis of Hodgson and Rachman (1974), that "concordance between response systems was likely to be high during strong emotional arousal". This hypothesis that "discordance will be more evident when emotional responses are relatively mild" was confirmed only so far as baseline assessments were concerned while, after Practolol or flooding, the increase in correlations during neutral stimuli did not confirm the hypothesis. As far as flooding was concerned, this could be due to this treatment having a global influence across different levels of arousal and, in this sense, the finding agreed with the observation that the efficacy of exposure treatment was independent of the amount of arousal elicited during treatment (Marks 1976). On the other hand, Practolol affected heart rate and probably G.S.R. measures indirectly through feedback connections regardless of the emotional loading of the stimuli.

The fact that the concordance and synchrony was more pronounced after flooding apart from confirming our first hypothesis set out above, indicated that the changes after treatment occured on both cognitive and autonomic levels in a way which affected the relationship between these two response systems. It could be suggested that the increase in the trends, rather than in the "positive-negative" dimension between these systems, might be indicative of some removal of inhibitory influence on the inter-level processes. Such inhibition might be imposed by avoidance learning (Hull 1943; Yates 1970).

Skin conductance measures appeared to produce higher correlations with subjective anxiety when compared to heart rate after flooding, during the high affect testing conditions. This partially confirmed the second hypothesis put forward above, as well as the assumption that G.S.R. by being a multi-system response, had a greater chance of being affected by the flooding therapy intervention. Nevertheless, this did not seem to be the case during neutral testing conditions and it could be suggested that this hypothesis was valid only beyond a certain level of arousal. Furthermore, this finding did not agree with the hypothesis of Hodgson and Rachman (1974) that "desynchrony between physiological and other measures will be greater for skin conductance than for heart rate". This could be due to the fact that the present data derived from population demonstrating active avoidance and this again could be seen in the light of the inter-level processes stated above. The probable importance of the latter might be deduced from the finding that high intercorrelations were elicited between G.S.R. measures after flooding. This suggested that increase in the intercorrelations, between different measures of the same response system, was likely to indicate a) its importance as a critical factor of improvement after a therapeutic intervention and b) its involvement in the avoidance learning under investigation.

Because Practolol produced desynchrony between subjective anxiety and heart rate, compared to baseline or after flooding, this confirmed the first part of the third hypothesis above. Nevertheless, desynchrony between G.S.R. measures and subjective anxiety was observed after Practolol so that the second part of this hypothesis was not confirmed. This might be attributed to the fact that Practolol did not enter the brain and so affect central autonomic mechanisms.

Regarding the last hypothesis, Practolol reduced intercorrelations between heart rate and spontaneous fluctuations compared with the baseline assessment, while, between heart rate and maximum deflection, the distribution of the correlations across the various testing conditions did not allow a definite confirmation of the hypothesis. However, after flooding an increase of intercorrelations between maximum deflection and spontaneous fluctuations and maximum deflection and heart rate was evident.

Finally, the data indicate that, in obsessive-compulsive patients, both heart rate and G.S.R. were sufficiently coupled with subjective anxiety changes, for them to be used as reliable indices of synchrony between these two response systems. The specific sensitivity of the G.S.R. measures found in these cases and its proposed superiority over heart rate, if confirmed, call for further exploration of synchrony under relevant and irrelevant stimulation. It was felt that such investigations might be useful in understanding the mechanisms and the regulatory processes operating in obsessive-compulsive neurosis.

SUMMARY

Sixteen patients suffering with obsessive-compulsive neurosis were placed on a three days' trial with a beta-blocker before undergoing flooding treatment. The latter consisted of ten two-hour sessions given twice weekly. Three identical psychophysiological assessments were carried out before the trial, after beta-blockade and after completion of the flooding therapy. The psychophysiological measures taken were of heart rate, skin conductance maximum deflection and spontaneous fluctuations, while subjective anxiety was recorded on a five point scale during the presentation of neutral and anxiety provoking testing conditions. The results suggest that flooding facilitates synchronous changes across physiological and subjective response systems. Higher correlations between these systems were also evident after flooding. In contrast, beta-blockade produces desynchrony between the measures employed. These findings are discussed and some hypotheses are put forward.

REFERENCES

Boulougouris J.C., Rabavilas A.D., and Stefanis C., (1977). Psychophysiological responses in obsessive-compulsive patients. Behaviour Research and Therapy, (in press).

Boulougouris, J.C., Rabavilas A.D., and Stefanis C., (1975). The effects of b-adrenergic blockers (Practolol) on psychophysiological measures in obsessional neurotics. Paper to the Conference on Dimensions of Anxiety and Stress, Oslo, June.

Hodgson R., and Rachman S., (1974). Desynchrony in measures of fear. Beha-viour Research and Therapy, 12, 319-326.

Hull, C.L., (1943). Principles of Behavior. Appleton-Century-Crofts, New York.

Lang P.J., Melamed, B.G., and Hart J., (1970). A psychophysiological analysis of fear modification using an automated desensitization procedure. Journal of Abnormal Psychology, 72, 220-234.

Lang P.J., (1971). The application of psychophysiological methods to the study of psychotherapy and behaviour modification. In A.E. Bergin and S.L. Garfield (Eds.) Handbook of Psychotherapy and Behaviour Change, Wiley, New York.'

Marks I.M. (1976). The current status of Behavioral Psychotherapy: Theory and Practice. American Journal of Psychiatry, 133:3 253-261.

Mowrer O.H. (1960). Learning Theory and Behavior. Wiley, New York.

Rachman S. (1976). The passing of the two-stage theory of fear and avoidance: fresh possibilities. Behaviour Research and Therapy, 14, 125-134.

Rachman S., and Hodgson R., (1974). Synchrony and Desynchrony in fear and avoidance. Behaviour Research and Therapy, 12, 311-318.

Yates, A.J. (1970). Behavior Therapy. Wiley, New York.

14. DRUGS IN TREATMENT OF OBSESSIONAL AND PHOBIC DISORDERS WITH BEHAVIOURAL THERAPY - POSSIBLE SYNERGISM

John Cobb

Institute of Psychiatry, London

It is nearly ten years since Fernandez and Lopez-Ibor (1967) suggested that clomipramine might be helpful in the management of obsessional neurosis. Since then the drug has been widely used in obsessional neurosis and to a lesser extent in phobic neurosis, and enthusiasm for its value has reached the point where some workers (e.g. Capstick, 1975) claim that the drug has "specific anti-obsessional" properties.

This paper has two aims. The first is to review the evidence supporting such claims. The second is to consider the value of comparing the effects of drugs in general and clomipramine in particular with the effects of behaviour therapy, as though the two approaches were competitive. This is an important question since some behaviour therapists might claim that their treatments are so effective in obsessional and phobic conditions that chemotherapy has become obsolete, just as some psychiatrists using physical treatments appear to be unaware of the value of behaviour therapy (Yaryura - Tobias 1975; Carey, 1975).

Reviewing the literature in an attempt to evaluate the value of drug treatment in these conditions has involved continual reference to the characteristics that might be sought in the "Perfect Study" Fig. 14.1.

THE "PERFECT" TREATMENT STUDY

1) Statement of aims.
2) Diagnostic purity.
3) Representative sample of adequate size.
4) Design   -: Double blind
           : Controls
           : Parallel or cross-over.
           : Independent assessor
5) Measures :- valid, reliable and appropriate.
6) Definition of specific treatment variables.
7) Control over non-specific treatment.
8) Definition of "outcome".
9) Adequate follow up.
10) Clarity of expression of results.
11) Inspired guesses.

Fig. 14.1   "The "Perfect" treatment study

No study ever satisfies all these criteria. Papers which report important clinical observations usually fall short on most grounds, but nonetheless have value in stimulating discussion and further research. A continual succession of uncontrolled reports, while adding a certain robustness to earlier observations, add nothing to their real validity. The literature concerning insulin coma therapy or carbon dioxide inhalation bears witness to this. Thus Carey (1975) in reporting an open label, uncontrolled study with a three week follow-up, concerning the effectiveness of clomipramine in phobic patients, adds little to the original case histories reported by van Renynghe de Voxvrie in 1968. Accumulating harder data by satisfying most of the "Perfect Study" criteria is a time-consuming business and only a few treatment trials involving drugs are of this standard (Tyrer, Candy and Kelly 1973: Tyrer and Steinberg, 1975: Solyom et al, 1973: Zitrin and Klein, 1975).

TREATMENT OF PHOBIC NEUROSIS

Simple tranquillisers, such as benzodiazepines are widely used in the treatment of all types of anxiety states, but their therapeutic effect is short-lived in phobic neurosis thus limiting their value (Marks, 1974). Case reports of the effectiveness of tricyclics in phobic states, imipramine (Klein 1964) and clomipramine (van Renynghe de Voxvrie 1968), together with reports of success using mono-amine oxidase inhibitors in similar conditions (Kelly, Guirguis, Frommer, Mitchell-Heggs and Sargant 1970), have led to three recent controlled studies. These studies show not only the advances that have been made, but also reveal the difficulties of working in this area.

TREATMENT OF PHOBIC CONDITIONS

STUDY	TYPES	TREATMENTS	RESULTS
Tyrer et al 1973 and 1975	Agoraphobic / Social phobic	1) Phenelzine 2) Placebo	Phenelzine > Placebo 1/12 for effect Difference significant to $p<0.05$ but small Relapse rate (25%) Non-specific factors
Solyom (1973)	Agoraphobics / Social phobics / Specific phobics	Flooding (F) Phenelzine/Brief Psychotherapy P.B.P. Placebo/Brief Psychotherapy Pl.B.P.	P.B.P. most rapid but high relapse Behaviour Therapy slower improvement relapse<10%
Zitrin (1975)	1. "Agoraphobics" 2. Phobic neurosis 3. Mixed phobics	Behaviour Therapy x Imipramine (BT) Behaviour Therapy x Placebo (BT) Supportive Psychotherapy x Imipramine (SP)	"Agoraphobics" and Mixed Phobics :- – Imipramine > Placebo S.P. >B.T. Phobic Neurosis :- – Imipramine = Placebo B.T. > S.P.

Fig. 14.2

Tyrer's study concerned 40 outpatients with either social phobia or agoraphobia of whom 32 completed the trial. At 2 years follow up he was only able to collect data from 70% of the original 40 patients. This study showed that phenelzine was significantly more effective than placebo (p < 0.05). Comparison with similar measures used in earlier studies of behavioural treatment (Gelder and Marks, 1968) showed the degree of improvement to be comparable with that produced by desensitisation in fantasy which is a weak and outdated behavioural method and less effective than exposure in-vivo. Several points need to be born in mind in interpreting these results.

In the first place, as in most controlled trials, this difference was found
in certain measures only, in this case those concerned with overall assessment
and second phobia, but not in measures of the main phobia, avoidance or social
adjustment. This result either means that the drug effect is weak and improves some symptoms but not others, or alternatively points to some research
design defect. Klein in 1964 suggested that drugs might lower anticipatory
anxiety (phobia rating) and not affect avoidance behaviour. This study and
the work of Solyom et al (1973) support this hypothesis.

Tyrer recognised that agoraphobic and socially phobic patients differ clinically and physiologically from other phobic patients, but assumed that his population of agoraphobic and social phobics were homogenous. If this assumption
is wrong, and clinical impression suggests it may be, then unresponsiveness
of one sub-group of patients may obscure a significant difference between
active treatment and placebo in the group as a whole. Similar criticism
applies to Solyom's study and only Zitrin (1975) has attempted to deal separately with phobic sub-groups. In addition, Tyrer paid no attention to the
acetylator status of his patients, which Johnstone and Marsh (1973) using
similar drug dosage (45 - 90 mgms. daily) have shown is important in determining the response of neurotic depression to phenelzine. Neither was he able
to measure blood levels of drug and its metabolites, which at least as far
as tricyclics are concerned may be an important factor in determining clinical
response (Asberg et al 1971). Both those factors may have minimised differences
between treatments, and this dilution effect may well acoount for Tyrer's
failure to find a difference on measures of primary phobias, while possibly
increasing the significance of the difference found on secondary phobias.

Placebo treatment improved patients considerably on phobic and avoidance
ratings and this improvement continued during the follow up period. It is
worth taking a closer look at this "placebo effect"which suggests that potent
non-specific therapeutic factors were operative in both groups, recognised
but uncontrolled by the therapists. Gelder and his associates (1973) has
already drawn attention to these non-specific factors. There is no reason
why they should not make a similar contribution to drug treatments. Important
among non-specific factors are; 1) the subject's expectations; 2) his preparation for treatment; 3) the duration and quality of personal contact;
4) the opportunity to practice counter-phobic behaviour between sessions
("homework"). The latter may be encouraged formally by the therapist, or
prompted by informal contact with other patients, and may be so powerful
as to swamp the contribution of specific therapeutic strategy under study
(Mathews, Johnston, Lancashire, Munby, Shaw and Gelder 1976).

The careful design was rewarded in this study by the finding that phenelzine
only became superior to placebo in the second month of treatment. Had the
treatment period only lasted one month, there would have been no difference.
Finally, the importance of follow-up was emphasised, since withdrawal of drug
was shown to lead to a high relapse rate. Other studies concerning drug
treatment of either phobic or obsessional states also comment on relapse following drug withdrawal (Marshal, 1971, Walter, 1973) which in Solyom's study
(1973) reached 100%. The implication of these findings is that patients
need to continue on drugs indefinitely in order to maintain any improvement.

Solyom and his associates (1973), studied 50 outpatients, a mixed group
containing agoraphobics, social phobics and specific phobics. They were allo-

cated to one of five treatment modalities. Three of these were behavioural, systematic desensitisation in fantasy, aversion relief and in vivo flooding. The other two were combined Brief Psychotherapy and Phenelzine or Brief Psychotherapy and Placebo. It is easy to criticise this asymetric design and thus difficult to draw firm conclusions from his results. On the one hand specific phobias are known to be easier to treat than agoraphobias (Gelder et al 1973) and on the other hand, in-vivo exposure has been shown to be more effective than fantasy exposure (Marks, 1974). Behavioural treatments cannot be lumped together as though all were equally effective. Furthermore, it is unsound to compare behaviour therapy with no tablet, with supportive psychotherapy and phenelzine/placebo. Also no mention is made of many potent non-specific factors which may have been operative.

Results again showed phenelzine to be superior to placebo. In the drug treatment group anxiety reduction preceded phobia reduction, whereas in the group having behaviour therapy the reverse was found (i.e. avoidance diminished before the feeling of anxiety provoked by anticipation). This is in keeping with Klein's hypothesis of drug action in phobias and is very relevant when considering the possibility of synergism between drugs and behavioural treatments. Finally, the combination of phenelzine and brief-psychotherapy had a more rapid action than "behaviour therapy". The results of both treatments were the same in the long run, though drug withdrawal led to 100% relapse while the relapse rate after "behaviour therapy" was less than 10%.

Zitrin's study (1975) is still incomplete and the published findings represent preliminary data. The design of the study suggests three forms of phobic disorder, in contrast to the two previous studies. Since there are three treatment modalities the study has a 3 x 3 design. Even with a relatively common disorder, to accumulate and treat nine groups of patients of sufficient size to make the study statistically sound, is a major undertaking. Although this study would have been more balanced if some form of placebo behaviour therapy had been involved, this would have meant a further increase in the patient sample. The preliminary finding indicating the superiority of supportive psychotherapy over desensitisation in fantasy clearly indicates that at least in Zitrin's hands psychotherapy is not the placebo that ardent behaviourists would have us believe! This study uses imipramine (a tricyclic) rather than phenelzine (a monoamine oxidase inhibitor), an important clinical difference. Tricyclics have fewer side effects and patients on them are not subject to irksome dietary restrictions. The design allows assessment of synergism between behaviour therapy and chemotherapy. Preliminary results show that imipramine is superior to placebo both in agoraphobic and mixed phobic groups, though not in simple phobics. In the same groups the combination of supportive psychotherapy and imipramine is slightly superior to the combination of desensitisation in fantasy and imipramine. In contrast the phobic neurosis group, shows no difference between imipramine and placebo, though desensitisation in fantasy gave better results than supportive therapy.

It is too early to draw definite conclusions from these results, and again non-specific factors such as homework were not controlled. However, the results support the possibility that there is no overall optimum strategy for all phobic states.

Summing up, there is evidence that tricyclics and MAOIS have significant effect in phobic states, though the only study in which similar measures were

used (Tyrer et al 1973) suggests that the amount of improvement is less than
that achieved by the most effective behavioural techniques, that is those
techniques involving exposure in-vivo. However, there are indications that
the effects of drugs and behavioural treatments may be synergistic and
certainly no evidence to show that they are antagonistic. In the present
state of knowledge, there is no evidence to show that any one drug is superior
to another. Taking other clinical considerations into account a tricyclic
such as imipramine or clomipramine is to be preferred.

TREATMENT OF OBSESSIONAL STATES

Primary obsessional neurosis is a rare condition with a prevalence of between
1 and 2% in patients under psychiatric care (Kringlen, 1965). Even this may
be an over-estimate since many studies include patients who have obsessional
symptoms secondary to a depressive illness and also patients with obsessional
personalities who have become depressed or anxious. Shortage of patients
makes it very difficult to undertake a properly controlled, double-blind study of treatment. To date, all the reports concerning drug treatment are open-
label, uncontrolled studies or simple case reports. Several include both
primary and secondary obsessional neurosis. Virtually all concerned the tricyclic drug, namely clomipramine. Activity of other tricyclic drugs has not
been compared, neither have drugs from other psycho-active groups. Probably
the main reason for this is that prior to 1967 obsessional neurosis had the
reputation of frustrating all treatment except leucotomy. Thus news of a
dramatic breakthrough was greeted with great enthusiasm. Furthermore, initial
reports suggested that the drug was more effective if given intravenously
(Beaumont, 1973). Other tricyclics with which it could have been compared
were not available for intravenous use, and thus it was not possible to do a
simple cross-over trial comparing clomipramine with other tricyclics.

Attempts have been made to compare oral and i.v. use (Beaumont, 1973). Considering the powerful placebo effect of i.v. infusions, it is hardly surprising
that these uncontrolled studies showed that the response to i.v. infusion was
superior to oral administration. Ethically it would be difficult to justify
giving i.v. infusions of placebo, thus a controlled trial is unlikely to be
done. Clomipramine is well absorbed orally though higher initial levels of
both clomipramine and its clinically active N-desmethy metabolite may be achieved by administration of the same dose intravenously (Faigle and Dieterle,
1973). However, this quantitative difference disappears about six hours after
administration. Maintenance on oral medication is said to be satisfactory
and moreover relapses respond well to oral rather than i.v. medication. One
of the four patients reported by Capstick in 1975, who on non-clinical grounds
was given oral rather than i.v. medication, responded as well as the other
three patients who were given infusions. In practice troublesome side effects,
especially haemoglobinuria, venous thrombosis and epileptiform seizures (Rack,
1973; Marshal and Micev, 1973) have led to a waning enthusiasm for intravenous
use and most recent reports have concerned oral use. (Yaryura - Tobias, 1975;
Carey, 1975). The reputation acquired through intravenous use has carried
over to the drug in capsule form, and by either route it is still seen by
many clinicians, as having unique properties.   Comments made earlier, concerning hard and soft data apply to treatment of obsessional neurosis as much
as to phobias, yet a wealth of clinical experience from different workers
in different countries cannot be lightly dismissed.   Some workers argue

that controlled trials are unnecessary. They point out that obsessional
neurosis is a chronic condition running a steady unremitting course. An
abrupt and impressive change in these symptoms, associated closely in time
with the administration of clomipramine, must, it is argued, be caused by
the drug. This argument can be challenged on several counts.

In the first place many of the reports concern patients who were depressed
and had had symptoms of short duration, and in general these were the patients
who did best. Thus it could be argued that this clinical improvement was the
result of an antidepressant rather than an anti-obsessional effect.

Although standard psychiatric texts support the view that obsessional neurosis
is extremely chronic, a review of the literature does not substantiate such a
pessimistic view Fig. 14.3.

OBSESSIONAL NEUROSIS PROGNOSIS

STUDY	F/U	PATIENTS	CURED / MUCH IMPROVED
Lewis (1936)	5 years	50	46 %
Langfeldt (1938)	1-11 years	27	30 % "quite healthy"
Muller (1957)	20-30 years	54	about 1/2
Rudin (1953)	2-5 years	102	about 1/3
Pollitt (1957)	3/12-15 years	105	leucotomized 60 % non-leucotomized 45 %
Ingram (1961)	1-11 years	89	leucotomized 55 % non-leucotomized 39 %
Kringlen (1965)	13-20 years	100	19 %

Fig. 14.3.

Furthermore, Kringlen (1965) showed that spontaneous remissions sometimes occured in the period following discharge from hospital. Fig. 14.4.

Type of Development of Illness

	Male	Female	Total
Unchanged since onset ..	10	16	26
Steady improvement after some years without improvement..	11	12	23
Varying without complete remission	5	13	18
Phasic course with symptom-free intervals	3	3	6
Steady worsening	1	5	6
Constant improvement ..	3	2	5
Ups and downs, but generally worsening	1	—	1
Information unreliable ..	4	2	6
Total	38	53	91

(KRINGLEN E. 1965)

Fig. 14.4.

Such remissions are not common and when they do occur are typically gradual. Fluctuations in the natural course may contribute but are unlikely to account for all the improvements associated with clomipramine therapy.

Another possible explanation is that some other incidental variable, such as staff enthusiasm, interaction between patients with similar problems, or the powerful placebo effect of intravenous medication might be responsible.   In other words, one of the non-specific factors mentioned in the previous section. It is possible that staff involved in treating and rehabilitating these patients were, without being aware of it, using what behaviourists would term modelling, exposure and response prevention in their day to day management. Marshall and Micev (1973) comment "as soon as fear began to be replaced by a sense of at least tranquility, and sometimes by what some described as adventureousness, patients were encouraged to undertake things which had previously caused discomfort".   These techniques have been shown (Marks, Hodgson, Rachman 1975; Boulougouris 1976) to produce a level of improvement in obsessional neurosis, at least equal to that claimed by workers with clomipramine.

Lacking a properly controlled trial, no firm conclusions can be drawn from the published literature on the drug treatment of obsessional neurosis, though several important observations can be made.

1. Obsessional neurosis no longer deserves the reputation it had ten years ago, as an untreatable condition.

2. Patients who have improved on drug therapy tend to relapse if the drug is withdrawn (Capstick, 1975), whereas those who have had behaviour therapy maintain their improvement. (Marks et al 1975; Rabavilas, Boulougouris and Stefanis 1976).

3. Several workers comment on the important inter-relation between obsessional symptomatology and close personal relationships. Symptom removal may lead to marital disruption (Marshall and Micev 1973; Walter 1973) and alternatively, domicilary treatment and marital work may enhance the effects of treatment (Marks, Hodgson, Rachman 1971 Stern and Marks, 1973).

4. From the treatment point of view, patients with obsessional compulsive neurosis cannot be considered to be homogenous group. Chemotherapy (Capstick, 1971: Walter 1973) and exposure in vivo (personal observation) are both more effective in obsessional rituals than in ruminations. Rabavilas et al (1976) in a sophisticated study, showed that different types of patients responded consistently to different types of exposure in-vivo. Rigby and his associates (1973) suggested that clomipramine was effective in some individuals but not in others, but was unable to identify any prognostic factors.

IS CLOMIPRAMINE DIFFERENT FROM OTHER TRICYCLICS

Work so far reviewed provides good evidence that both monoamine oxidase inhibitors and tricyclics have some effect on phobic disorders. The evidence supporting the effectiveness of clomipramine in obsessional disorders is less soundly based, but is sufficient to prompt the question as to whether or not clomipramine is different from other tricyclics.

STRUCTURE

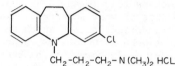

CHLORPROMAZINE

IMIPRAMINE

CLOMIPRAMINE

AMITRIPTYLINE

Fig. 14.5

It is worth recalling that the so-called "tricyclics" are a heterologous group of drugs whose generic name is misleading since not all contain three rings though all are used in similar treatment situations. Conventional drug classification is at times arbitrary and phenothiazines in general are quite like some tricyclics in structure. Chlorpromazine and clomipramine both have a three ringed structure with an attached chlorine atom, while clomipramine looks structurally quire unlike amitriptyline.

PHARMACOLOGY

It is well established that both noradrenaline and 5 hydroxytryptamine are central nervous system synaptic transmitters and the most significant neurochemical effect of tricyclics is believed to be their potency in inhibiting uptake of N.A. and 5 HT at pre-synaptic terminals. Tricyclics may be ranged along a spectrum, with those whose effect is mainly on 5 HT at one end and those whose effect is mainly on N.A. at the other Fig. 14.6

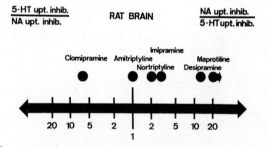

Fig. 14.6.   Relative potencies of antidepressants in inhibiting serotonin and noradrenaline uptake (for explanation see text).

FROM WALDMEIER *ET AL.* (1976)

Clomipramine is the most specific inhibitor of 5 HT uptake and has the weakest
effect on N.A. uptake (Horn 1976). Since the exact roles of N.A. and 5 HT in
mediating mood and behaviour is not known, the clinical significance of this
difference is uncertain.

Interest has recently been directed towards the relationship between plasma
prolactin levels and mental function. Clomipramine has been shown to elevate
plasma prolactin, whereas amitriptyline has no effect (Francis et al 1976).
Chlorpromazine also inhibits 5 HT uptake and raises plasma prolactin, and in
these respects resembles clomipramine.

All tricyclics depress R.E.M. sleep, but clomipramine is the most potent of
the group in this respect (Oswald, 1975).

In view of these pharmacological differences, it is surprising that controlled
trials which have compared the clinical effects of clomipramine with other
tricyclics in cases of depressive illness have failed to show any significant
differences. Symes (1967) and Rack (1973), compared clomipramine with imipramine and found both equally effective as antidepressants, with no difference
in the speed of onset and no difference in side effects. This result cannot
be transferred directly to phobic and obsessional states, however, since
several workers (e.g. Tyrer et al 1973) have shown that improvement in phobic
ratings in patients on "antidepressants" is not correlated with improvement
in depression ratings. Tricyclics are known to have sedative effects and
Zitrin (1975) observed that imipramine appeared to achieve its effect through
eliminating spontaneous panic attacks rather than through an antidepressant
action. The possibility remains that the unique pharmacological properties
of clomipramine may yet be shown to be reflected in its clinical action.

CONCLUSION

In the present state of knowledge it is clear that the use of behaviour therapy in the management of phobic and obsessional states is well established,
though the evidence supporting the value of behaviour therapy is based on
much harder data than that supporting the value of drugs. Possibly drugs
act by reducing unpleasant emotional states such as anxiety and panic, associated with these conditions, whereas behaviour therapy leads to a lasting
reduction in avoidance. If this is so, it is likely that in the future the
optimum therapeutic strategy will be shown to be a combination of both techniques.

Cost effectiveness has not been discussed in detail in this paper. Whereas
it may be more convenient in practical terms to write a prescription, drugs
are expensive, have side effects and may have to be continued indefinitely.
Behaviour therapy does require training of personnel, though nurses can
acquire the necessary skills after 18 months specialised training (Marks 1975).

Clomipramine has some unique pharmacological properties. It is as effective
as other drugs, but there are no good reasons for believing it to be superior.

It is easy to criticise past studies and to enumerate the difficulties in ob-
taining and interpreting data. Even the best study has its shortcomings.
In order to get the best return for investment of time and money, it is essen-

tial in future studies to plan carefully with these criticisms in mind.

ACKNOWLEDGEMENTS

The author wishes to thank Dr. I.M. Marks and Dr. J. Crammer for their invaluable advice.

REFERENCES

Asberg, M. Cronholm, B., Sjoqvist F. and Tuck, D. (1971). Relationship between plasma level and therapeutic effect of nortriptyline. British Medical Journal, 3, 331-334.

Beaumont, G. (1973). Clomipramine (Anafranil) in the treatment of obsessive-compulsive disorders - A review of the work of Dr. G.H. Collins. Journal of International Medical Research, 1, 423-424.

Boulougouris, J.C. (1976). Variables affecting the behaviour modification of obsessive compulsive patients treated by flooding. Paper presented at the Sixth Annual conference of E.A.B.T., Spetsae.

Capstick, N. (1975). Clomipramine in the treatment of the true obsessional state - A report on four patients. Psychosomatics, 16, (1), 21-5.

Carey, M.S. (1975). The use of clomipramine in phobic patients. Preliminary Research Report. Current Therapeutic Research, 17, (1), 107-10.

Francis, A.F., Williams, P., Williams, R., Link, G., Zole, E.N. and Hughes, D. (1976). The effect of clomipramine on prolactin levels - Pilot studies, Postgraduate Medical Journal, Supplement 3, 52, 87-92.

Gelder, M.G. and Marks, (1968). Desensitisation and Phobias: a crossover study. British Journal of Psychiatry, 114, 323-328.

Gelder, M.G., Bancroft J.H.J., Gath, D.H., Johnston, D.W., Mathews, A.M., and Shaw, P.M., (1973). Specific and non-specific factors in behaviour therapy British Journal of Psychiatry, 123, 445-462.

Horn, A.S., (1976). The interaction of tricyclic antidepressants with the biogenic amine uptake systems in the central nervous syteem. Postgraduate Medical Journal, Supplement 3, 52, 25-31.

Faigle, J.W. and Dieterle, W. (1973). The metabolism and pharmacokinetics of clomipramine. Journal of International Medical Research, 1-5, 281-290.

Johnstone, E. and Marsh, W. (1973). Acetylater status and response to Phenelzine in depressed patients. Lancet, 1, 567-570.

Kelly, D. Guirguis, W., Frommer, E., Mitchell-Heggs, N. and Sargant W. (1970). Treatment of phobic states wtth antidepressants: a retrospective study of 246 patients. British Journal of Psychiatry, 116, 387-398.

Klein, D.F. (1964). Delineation of two drug-responsive anxiety syndromes. Psychopharmacologia Berlin, 5, 397-408.

Kringlen, E. (1965). Obsessional neurotics: A long term follow-up. British Journal of Psychiatry, 111, 709-722.

Lopez-Ibor and Fernandez (1967). Monochlorimipramine in the treatment of psychiatric patients resistent to other therapies. Act. Luso. Esp. Neurol., 26, 119-147.

Marks, I.M., Hodgson, R. Rachman S. (1975). Treatment of chronic obsessive-compulsive neurosis by in-vivo exposure. British Journal of Psychiatry, 127, 349-365.

Marks, I.M., (1974). Research in neurosis: A selective review. Psychological Medicine 4, 1, 89-109.

Marks, I.M., (1975). Nurse therapists in behavioural psychotherapy. British Medical Journal iii, 144-148.

Marks, I.M. et al (1976). In preparation.

Marshall, W.K., (1971). Treatment of obsessional illnesses and phobic anxiety states with Clomipramine. British Journal of Psychiatry, 119, 467-468.

Marshall, W.K., and Micev, V. (1973). Clomipramine in the treatment of obsessional illness and phobic anxiety states. Journal of International Medical Research, 1, 5, 403-412.

Mathews, A.M., Johnston, D.W., Lancashire, M., Munby M., Shaw, P.M., and Gelder M.G. (1976). Imaginal flooding and exposure to real phobic situations: Treatment outcome with agoraphobic patients. British Journal of Psychiatry, 129, 362-71.

Oswald, I. (1973). Sleep studies with clomipramine and related drugs. Journal or International Medical Research, 1, 296-298.

Rabavilas, A.D., Boulougouris J. C., and Stefanis C. (1976). Duration of flooding sessions in the treatment of obsessive-compulsive patients. Behaviour Research and Therapy, 14, 349-355.

Rack, P.H. (1973). Clomipramine in the treatment of obsessional states with special reference to the Leyton Obsessional Inventory. Journal of International Medical Research, 1, 5, 332 and 397-402.

Renynghe De Voxvrie, G. van (1968). Anafranil in obsessive neurosis. Acta Neurologica et Psychiatrica Belgica, 68, (8), 787-92.

Rigby, B., Clarren S., and Kelly, D. (1973). A Psychological and physiological evaluation of the effects of intravenous clomipramine. Journal of International Medical Research. 308-316.

Stern, R. and Marks, I.M. (1973). Contract therapy in obsessive compulsive neurosis with marital discord. British Journal of Psychiatry, 123, 577, 681-684.

Solyom, L., Heseltine, G.F., McClare, D.J., Solyom, C., Ledwidge, B. and Steinberg, G. (1973). Behaviour therapy versus drug therapy in the treatment of phobic neurosis. Canadian Psychiatric Association Journal 18, 25-32.

Symes (1967). Monochlorimipramine: A controlled trial of a new antidepressant. British Journal of Psychiatry, 113, 671-675.

Tyrer, P., Candy, J., and Kelly, D. (1973). Phenelzine in phobic anxiety: a controlled trial. Psychological Medicine, 3, 120-124.

Tyrer, P. and Steinberg, D. (1975). Symptomatic treatment of agoraphobia and social phobias: A follow-up study. British Journal of Psychiatry, 27, 163-168.

Waldmeier, P.C., Baumann, P., Greengrass, P.M. and Maitre, L. (1976). Effects of clomipramine and other tricyclic antidepressants on biogenic amine uptake and turnover. Postgraduate Medical Journal, 52 (Supplement 3), 33-39.

Walter, C.J.S., (1973). Clinical impressions on treatment of obsessional states with intravenous clomipramine. Journal of International Medical Research, 1, 5, 413-416.

Yaryura-Tobias, J.A. (1975). The action of clomimipramine in obsessive-compulsive neurosis: A pilot study. Current Therapeutic Research, 17, (1), 111-116.

Zitrin, C.M., and Klein D.F., (1975). Imipramine, behaviour therapy and phobias. Psychopharmacology Bulletin 11, 4, 41-2.

AUTHOR INDEX

A

Agras, W.S., 14, 18, 19, 41, 46, 63
Akhtar, S., 85, 97
Allen, R., 14, 19
Alt, B., 21, 38
Amatu, H.T., 16, 20
Asberg, M., 129, 136
Ashcroft, J.B., 103, 104
Azrin, N., 108, 113

B

Bancroft, J.H.J., 1, 5, 73, 83, 130, 136
Bandura, A., 56,62
Barlow, D.H., 14, 18, 63
Bassiakos, L., 56,62, 66, 70, 74, 83
Baum, M., 65, 62
Baumann, P., 134, 138
Beaumont, 131, 136
Beck, A.T., 7, 12, 22, 38
Beech, H.R., 79, 81, 82, 95, 97
Benjamin, S., 45, 46
Berlyne, D.E., 79, 81
Blakey, R.S., 16, 20
Boersma, K., 96, 97
Bohnert, M., 7, 12
Borcovec, T.D., 18
Boulougouris, J.C., 56, 62, 66, 70, 73 74, 76, 79, 82, 83, 115, 116 124, 133, 136, 137
Bowers, K.S., 79,83
Bradshaw, P.W., 103, 104
Brand, J., 25, 38
Bruer, J., 25, 38
Burns, L. E., 16, 20
Butollo, W. H., 21, 25, 38
Butz, R., 14, 19

C

Callahan, E.J., 22, 38
Cameron, R., 9, 12, 26, 38
Candy, J., 128, 138
Capstick, N., 127, 131, 133, 136
Carey, M.S., 127, 131, 136
Cauthen, N.P., 14, 19
Chesser, E.S., 68, 70
Clarren, S., 133, 137
Cohen-Kettenis, P., 14, 18
Cooper, A., 86, 94, 97
Cronholm, B., 129, 136
Crow, M., 14, 18

D

Dekker, J., 81, 97
Den Hengst, S., 85, 97
Dieterle, W., 131, 136
Di Loreto, A.O., 16, 18
D' Zurilla, T.J., 16, 18

E

Edwards, J., 14, 19
Emmelkamp, P.G.M., 3, 5, 13, 14, 15, 18, 19, 97, 105, 113
Emmelkamp-Benner A., 15, 19
Everaerd, W.T.A.M., 14, 19
Eysenck, H.J., 102, 104

F

Faigle, J.W., 131, 136
Fedoravicios, A., 16, 19

SUBJECT INDEX